D0574863

MUSIC DISTRIBUTION
SELLING MUSIC IN THE NEW ENTERTAINMENT MARKETPLACE

A complete guide to Music Distribution, Marketing, Promotions and Selling Music.

C. Michael Brae
with Dameon V. Russell

Bonus Marketing Section
Chapter11 - written by Dameon V. Russell

C. Michael Brae - CEO/Hitman Records, Instructor-San Francisco State University (Music Recording Industry Program) and UCLA (Entertainment Studies)

Dameon V. Russell – COO/Hitman Records, Inc., Managing Member DeFor Investment Group Llc, guest lecturer San Francisco State University (Music Recording Industry Program) and UCLA (Entertainment Studies)

MUSIC DISTRIBUTION
OVERVIEW

This Book is a comprehensive study of the record industry distribution system. It has a "real" hands-on approach with current projects already in motion within the distribution system, in conjunction with the distribution A&R department. Distribution is but one aspect of the business end of this industry, arguably the most vital. The importance of distribution is stressed along with the importance of other contiguous aspects such as sales, marketing, and promotions-including music-video, radio, retail, trades, consumer print, street-promotions, and college-networks. Marketing through cutting-edge web-technology, and how to incorporate into retail distribution networks supporting soundscan capabilities, is discussed. In general terms the text within very specifically details the functionality of music distribution and the components and variables that facilitate that functionality. The product distribution systems, wholesale/retail markups, pricing strategies, major chains, rack jobbers, one-stops, mom and pop stores, and other retail outlets are also examined. Included will be a campaign on existing product already within retail systems—and examining radio promotion campaign efforts on targeted markets through telephone tracking methods.

The basic necessity of distribution is a product of fulfillment. Meeting mounting consumer demand derived of external marketing and promotion results, but doing so in a preemptive methodology. In this book you will find that methodology prefaced, defined, detailed and justified. The intent is to convey total understanding of the process of music distribution as well as the significance of that process and all it's variables in the scheme of the business of music.

CONTENTS

APPENDIX

1. Performing Rights Organizations
2. Trade Publications
3. College Radio Stations
4. Template: Radio Tracking Report Code Sheet
5. Template: Radio Tracking Report
6. Template: Distribution Agreement
7. Template: Distribution Agreement -Production/Manufacture/Distribution
8. Template: Management Contract
9. U.S. Radio Market Data Spreadsheet

GLOSSARY

Glossary of Music and Industry Related Terms

ABOUT THE AUTHORS

C. Michael Brae is currently CEO, Chairman and Founder of Hitman Records and also teaches *Record Distribution* and *Marketing* at San Francisco State University in the (Music Recording Industry Program) along teaching *Selling Music in the New Entertainment Marketplace* at UCLA (Entertainment Studies).

Hitman Records began in 1991 and solidified a joint venture with SOLAR (Sounds of Los Angeles Records) in 1995. Mr. Brae worked with SOLAR under President and General Counsel, Virgil Roberts, and secured distribution for Hitman Records through a distributor of SOLAR, INDI.

In 1997, Hitman Records switched distributors to Bayside Distribution. The record label then began a period of artist acquisition and development, which focused on hip-hop, rap, r&b and gospel genres. During this period, Mr. Brae represented well-known and established artists, such as Samuelle (double-platinum and Grammy award winning singer for the r&b group Club Nouveau) and Mac Dash Mone (former member of the double-platinum group Digital Underground).

A native New Yorker, Mr. Brae began his career on Wall Street after graduating with a double Bachelors degree in marketing and advertising from the University of San Francisco. Having had strong sales, marketing strategies and new business development, Mr. Brae secured high profile corporate companies such as Delta Airlines, Bell Atlantic and Standard Motor Products producing up to 65% increased revenue in achieving goals at previous companies.

Hitman Records has a number of diversified layered revenue streams. The degree of both vertical and horizontal integration allows Hitman Records to generate revenue through commissions and management fees throughout the entire development and sales cycle of the product. The focus of selling business to business and business to consumer will provide leverage.

6

Dameon V. Russell

Dameon V. Russell is the Cofounder and Managing Member of DeFor Investment Group, LLC; a private real estate investment and development firm and Small Business Administration certified 8(a) Government Contractor. Mr. Russell began his real estate career over a decade ago in the business of Discounted Trust Deeds. Over a four-year period he closed transactions totaling more than $61 million worth of loans encumbering real property in eleven states. He has facilitated transactions involving a broad scope of financial institutions including First Franklin, Berkeley Federal, GE Capital, Home Savings of America, Sumitomo Bank and FSB Mortgage Corporation. Mr. Russell's experience has enabled him to master skills of analysis, conduct of due diligence and negotiation. Combined with his educational background in marketing strategies and implementation and his intuitive natural ability to "get things done", Mr. Russell has proven to be an invaluable member of Hitman Records' executive management team. Mr. Russell has a profound understanding of trends, and market diversities pertaining to all music genres, and an ability to conduct sound demographic market analysis. More note worthy is his skill at converting such data to strategy, and subsequently to revenue.

Dedicated to those we love both here and that have gone ahead. Equally dedicated to those Indies striving to fulfill a self-determined destiny, we wish to see you succeed in that endeavor; use this book to that end.

CHAPTER 1

MUSIC INDUSTRY STUDY AND FACTS

Statement of fact; 27,000 titles were released in the 2001 calendar year. This includes all releases from major labels, independent labels, new releases as well as re-releases. Once you can conceive of that number, you will realize the competition with other titles in the marketplace, product buy-in, positioning, relationships, pricing strategies, marketing campaigns, that factor into the success or failure of your project. The average retail outlet houses fewer than 3,500 titles. The overwhelming majority are what is commonly referred to as "deep catalog", everything from Elvis and the Temptations to Pink Floyd and Earth-Wind & Fire. Certain titles must always be stocked. A much smaller percentage of the inventory is reserved for new titles, "hot product"; of these titles, the majority are major label releases. Clearly you can see how product placement at retail is crucial and achieving it is a difficult task.

We estimate that US consumer spending on recorded music will total about $17 billion by the end of 2003. The US recorded music industry is dominated by five distributors, whose recordings account for roughly 80% of retail sales. Those companies are: Vivendi-Universal, Sony, AOL/Time Warner, EMI Group and Bertelsmann.

Industry Trends- Long-term stability and growth in US entertainment discretionary spending depends heavily on the development of new ways of delivering films, television shows, and music to consumers. Successful new delivery systems generally should spur growth in demand for these types of entertainment product from distributors. Although cable television and home video have substantially increased both the demand for and the economic value of programming, these delivery systems are relatively mature. More than 80% of US homes have a VCR, and close to 70% subscribe to cable or satellite TV services.

Longer Hours- Collectively, in this age of telecommuting and the home office, as we progress steadily wayward of the 9 to 5 employment status quo, television executives have recognized and sought to exploit non-conventional time slots finding profitable viewership base even in late night hours. Conventional wisdom brought about the term "prime-time", 7:00 pm to 10:00 pm, assuming the dated event of the 6:00 pm dinner hour. The prime-time slot once a finite line, the revenue jewel of television broadcasting. The slot is still king, though society, cable broadcasting and the $1.99 movie rental have substantially blurred the line.

Air-time Availability-With thousands of national, regional and local television stations, and with extended programming hours, airtime is readily available. The growth of cable television, satellites, and super-stations has brought television broadcasting a long way since the time when CBS, NBC and ABC had predominant exclusivity of the airwaves. Cable advertising networks once the home of sometimes less than glossy, municipal or regional commercial spots, now reach millions of potential consumers and are now replete with major advertisers and national ad campaign spots. The end result is that smaller advertisers have an abundance of options and available airtime with national consumer viewership. This has changed the face and scope of television advertising dramatically.

Coverage- 98% of all US households have at least (1) television set. In this Electronic Age, TV has surpassed all other media as our primary source of information and entertainment. Television is no longer "just for entertainment", it hasn't been for quite some time. Even those US consumers who previously watched very little television, preferring instead the intimacy or knowledge exuded from a good book or the evening paper, even these individuals now find it difficult to ignore the tube. There are enormous amounts of quality, informative and content-rich hours of television programming available for their discerning consumption. Television simply covers it all in this day

10

and age.

Infomercials- Roughly 1/5 the costs of a 30-second commercial to produce and air on cable advertising networks. Although this forum got a bad rap in the late eighties and through the nineties with some less than reputable product pitches, no one can dispute their validity in terms of the success rate they for the most part enjoy in reaching a broad base of consumers. Some businesses have found that hiring a media buying firm is more convenient and less expensive than buying airtime directly. Media-buying firms purchase blocks of time in many areas of the country and allocate these time blocks to their clients with a slight mark up. These firms prepay networks for this time or reserve it at a locked price then look to resell it to their clientele. Such firms deal in radio airtime, and print ad space as well and are widely utilized in the music industry due the ability to acquire, television, print and radio advertising schedules based on demographic models to target and reach specific consumer groups in many markets.

Cost-Effective- Infomercial, and general Airtime costs are less than conventional mail order or print campaigns designed to reach a like number of potential consumers. Example: One half hour of Airtime at WNEU can reach over 200,000 homes in Pittsburgh, PA for around $200. An infomercial can be aired on cable stations that reach 60 million homes nationwide. Infomercials are an exciting new territory with NO boundaries.

Alternative Sales Approach- Increase your sales by 10%, reach over 28 million hearing impaired viewers and families. Over 10% of the US population is hard of hearing, along with families, friends, that's 70-million viewers. This may not seem relevant for music marketing, however, a substantial number, in fact the majority of these 28 million persons is not deaf, only hearing impaired and they are music product consumers.

Music Videos have become a valuable promotional tool

11

for the music industry. Labels supply the videos to the channels, such as MTV, VH-1, BET, and CMT, to *break* a new act or recording. In addition, video broadcasts appear to drive approximately 20% of all record sales. Labels and artists normally "split" the cost of producing the music videos. Artists are required to agree to perform in the videos and the label will agree to use the videos to promote the artist's image and sell recordings. Some major artists pay all production expenses in order to obtain sole copyright ownership of the finished video product. Later they package the videos as a video album for retail consumption in VHS and DVD format. Traditionally, videos fail to sell more than a few thousand copies: 50,000 units is considered a "gold" video release. The video release does have measurable positive residual impact on album sales.

MTV celebrated its 20th birthday in 2001. Many in the entertainment industry refer to those younger than 20 as "MTV babies," because MTV had a major impact on the way TV programs are produced. MTV pioneered the fast paced, "in your face" style of programming and advertising. With quick cuts, layered graphics, multiple messages, loud audios, high impact visuals, frenetic bursts, and random transitions, this style has affected programming of every media type and the affects are still being calculated today.
Did you know?

- MTV globally reaches 350 million households (*PBS On-Line, 2001*).

- MTV has been a very successful business because it is almost non-stop advertising. In addition to the traditional commercials the videos themselves promote new albums.

- 82% of MTV viewers are 12 to 34 years old, with 39% under the age of eighteen (*Nielson Media Research, 2000*)

- Music videos are designed for teenagers between 12 and 19 years of age (*Rich, 1998*).

- MTV is watched by 73% of boys and 78% of girls in the 12 to 19 years of age group. Boys watch for an average of 6.6 hours per week and girls watch for an average of 6.2 hours per week (*Rich, 1998*)

- MTV is the most recognized network among young adults ages 12 to 34 (*Nielson Media Research, 2000*)

Sexual Imagery, Violence, Alcohol and Tobacco Portrayal in Music Videos:

- In one study 75% of concept music videos (*those that told a story*) involve sexual imagery and more than half involve violence - usually against women (*Pediatrics, 2001*).

- An analysis of music videos found that nearly one-fourth of all MTV videos portray overt violence and depict weapon carrying with attractive role models being aggressors in more than 80% of the violent videos (*DuRant, 1997*).

- One-fourth of all MTV videos contain alcohol or tobacco use (*DuRant, 1997*).

- A longitudinal study found a positive correlation between TV and music video viewing and alcohol consumption among teens (*Robinson, 1998*).

The Effects

- According to some research even modest viewing of MTV and other music videos results in significant exposure to glamorized depictions of alcohol and tobacco use, alcohol use linked with sexuality, and violence and weapons.

- When lyrics are acted out in a story telling music video, their impact is enhanced.

- Music videos appear to contribute to teens' desensitization to violence.

- The use of violence by music video stars makes it normal and more acceptable.

13

- At least two experiments show that watching MTV results in more permissive attitudes about sex. One of these (*Calfin, Carroll, & Schmidt, 1993*) found that college students who were assigned to watch MTV developed more liberal attitudes toward premarital sex than their peers who did not watch MTV as part of the study. In the second (*Greeson & Williams, 1986*) found that seventh and ninth graders were more likely to approve of premarital sex after watching MTV for less than one hour.

What to do:

- Restrict viewing of MTV by younger children.

- Limit exposure to MTV and other music videos with older teens.

- Talk with your teen about what they are watching.

- Consider contacting your cable company and blocking access to music video channels.

Sources:
Calfin, M.S., Carroll, J. L., & Schmidt, J. (1993). Viewing music-video tapes before taking a test of premarital sexual attitudes. Psychological Reports, 72, 475-481.

DuRant, R. H. (1997). Tobacco and alcohol use behaviors portrayed in music videos: content analysis. American Journal of Public Health, 87, 1131-1135.

DuRant, R.H., Rich, M., Emans, S. J., Rome, E. S., Allred, E., Woods, E. R., (1997). Violence and weapon carrying in music videos: a content analysis. Pediatric Adolescent Medicine, 151, 443-448.

Greeson, L.E., & Williams, R.A. (1986). Social implications of music videos on youth: An analysis of the content and effects of MTV. Youth and Society, 18, 177-189.

Nielson Media Research (2000).

PBS On-Line (2001) with Todd Cunninham. Web site: http:www.PBS.org (visited 6/8/2001).

Pediatrics (2001, January). Sexuality, contraception and the media. 107, 191.

Rich, M., Woods, E., Goodman, E., Emans, J., DuRant, R. (1998, April). Aggressors or victims: gender and race in music video violence. Pediatrics, 101, 669-674.

Robinson, T. N. (1998). Television and music video exposure and risk of adolescent alcohol use. Pediatrics, 102, p5. Web site: http://www.pediatrics.org/cgi/content/full/102/5/e54 (visited 6/18/2001).

The international recording industry is producing more national repertoire than ever before, with seven out of every 10 records sold worldwide carrying music by local artists. New data released by IFPI, shows recordings by domestic artists and acts signed to local music labels have risen from 58% to 68% of sales between 1991 and 2000.

A decade of growth in local music across all regions, except Africa and the Middle East, is one of the key findings of IFPI's Recording Industry numbers in 2001, published by the trade organization of the international recording industry.

The Recording Industry in Numbers contains 200 pages of analysis, information and comment on 76 markets across all of the world's regions, including analysis by repertoire, sales channel, price point, genre and consumer age band.

2001's eighth edition also includes, for the first time: a comprehensive summary of key music market trends over the decade; commentary and analysis on the world's top 20 music markets; and an enhanced Appendix section containing CD player statistics and a timeline of events in the industry.

Jay Berman, Chairman and CEO of IFPI, said: "The recording industry in the past decade has emerged as a major investor in local culture worldwide. The industry continues to develop creative talent in all regions and countries of the world, and it is contributing more than ever to the success of local artists and to the development of national music cultures."

The Recording Industry in Numbers also shows:

- The success story of the CD, with sales up 150% over the decade. Sales have increased every year since the format was first introduced in 1983, including in 2000 when annual CD sales hit 2.5 billion.

- Cassettes accounted for more than half of all music sales ten years ago. Now less than one in four recordings sold worldwide is a cassette. Singles sales stayed roughly unchanged (*as a share the total*) over the decade.

- The UK comes out on top in terms of per capita consumption - with an average of four record purchases a year per person - followed by Denmark, USA, Norway, Switzerland, Sweden, Germany, Iceland, Australia and Japan.

- In 2000, Britney Spears, Santana and the Beatles featured in more national top ten album charts than any other artists (*in 19, 18 and 16 countries, respectively*).

- Rap, hip-hop and other forms of urban music are the fastest-rising music genres in major markets. In the USA and the UK (ranked 1 and 3 worldwide) rock and heavy metal accounted for one in four record sales in 2000, but the share of rap and hip-hop rose to 13% in the USA and doubled to 4% in the UK.

The Recording Industry World Sales 2000: CD albums up, overall unit sales down by 1.2%

London - April 19 2001, Global sales of recorded music fell by 1.3% in value and 1.2% in units in 2000, with a decline in North America and other regions offsetting improved album sales worldwide and a strong market performance in several countries in Europe.

The global music market was worth US $36.9 billion,

16

with total unit sales of 3.5 billion.

Sales in Europe rose by 1.4% in value and 1.3% in units, although individual territories showed mixed results, with Germany, France and Italy all feeling the impact of mass CD-R copying and piracy.

Sales of CD albums grew by 2.5% to 2.5 billion units, with a particularly strong increase in Europe (*5.1%*). Global sales of singles and cassettes fell by 14.3% and 9.4% respectively. The availability of free online file-sharing services had clear repercussions for singles sales in the world's largest market, the United States, where there was a sharp 46% drop.

There was a mixed picture in Asia (*down 4.4% in value*) and Latin America (*down 1.0% in value*), regions which both suffer from high levels of piracy.

The figures were released today by IFPI, the organization representing the global recording industry. IFPI's membership numbers more than 1,400 record producers and distributors in over 70 countries.

Commenting on the figures Jay Berman, IFPI chairman and CEO said: "Last year was a mixed picture for the global recording industry. The downturn in the USA brought down the overall sales figures. On the other hand, CD album sales continued to rise worldwide. We also saw the first evidence of the impact of free online music, as well as the damage being done by unauthorized CD-R copying in some major markets.

"At the same time significant progress was made towards realizing the huge potential of the legitimate online music market. This is becoming apparent with recent announcements, including ventures such as Duet and MusicNet, which signal our members' determination to develop this area of business."

North America
The United States, which represents 38% of the total world music market, saw a decline in value of 1.5% and in units of 4.7% - reflecting a sharp reduction in sales of both cassettes and singles. In the US, the sales trend for CD singles has been a gradual decline

17

over the past three years. In 2000 however, there was a dramatic 39% fall in sales of CD singles, which was attributable in part to the availability of free online music.

The decline in sales in the USA in 2000 follows two exceptionally strong years for repertoire and releases. With Canada also seeing a fall in sales in 2000, North America as a whole was down 4.8% in units and 1.8% in value.

Europe
Music sales in both western and Eastern Europe varied across the region. The UK saw an increase of 3.8% in value from increased unit sales of 6.2% while France and Germany were both down 1.2% in value and the Italian market fell 4.1%. These three countries report a marked increase in CD-R copying and piracy.

Scandinavian countries were buoyant as a whole, with Denmark and Sweden up in units by 6.5% and 6.6% respectively.

Asia
In Asia, the market fell by 4.4% in value, despite an increase in units of 1.2%. In Japan, a rise in unit sales of 2.5% was accompanied by a 4.5% loss in value, the market being affected by a large number of releases of low-cost compilation albums.

Elsewhere in Asia, the higher rates of growth seen in South Korea, Hong Kong and India were more than offset by a downturn in China, Philippines and Taiwan - all suffering from very high rates of music piracy.

Latin America
Sales fell in 2000 for the third time, though less acutely than in the previous two years. In value terms, the region's market fell only slightly, by 1.0%, though unit sales were down by 3.3%, mirroring the ongoing format transfer from cassette to CD.

Brazil, the largest Latin American market, showed growth of 7.6% in units and 9.3% in value but the increases reflect recovery from a disastrous 1999 and do not signal any major reversal in the country's chronic piracy problem. Mexico, the second largest market in the region, and also severely hit by piracy, was down in units.

Other markets
Sales in Australia were down - by almost 2% in units and 4.2% in value. Overall, sales in the Middle East were down, by 3.9% in units, 2.1% in value, though there was growth in individual countries such as Turkey, Oman and Bahrain.

Related information from http://www.riaa.com

Welcome to the record business, where giant corporations risk more than $1 billion each year on young, untested musicians whose careers typically crash and burn. The few who do succeed contribute truckloads of cash to industry coffers. Profits from blockbuster releases by such acts as 'N Sync and Hootie & the Blowfish help companies offset losses from thousands of failures each year. For every successful act such as the Spice Girls, there are nine bands like the rock group Radish--signed for a ton of money and touted as the next big thing--that never make it.

There are the millions in marketing and promotion lost on pop acts such as Take Five, which disappeared in a blink, and a seemingly endless list of promising hopefuls such as rock band Gwen Mars, hip-hop act Major Figgas and R&B singer Sammy. This is the record industry's defense in a controversy now winding its way through the courts and in a debate with activist artists who are challenging the economics of the record business.

Company practices have come under scrutiny by lawmakers after some stars complained recently to Congress that the industry uses unconscionable contracts and corrupt accounting tactics to rob artists of their share of earnings. But the record companies say that just isn't so. According to the major labels, it's the artists who are making out like bandits. Major label executives decided to come forward after articles in the Los Angeles Times detailed efforts by rock star Courtney Love and others to break their contracts and organize an artists trade group to fight the Big Five music conglomerates.

Pop music, executives say, is a high-risk, low-margin business in which more than 90% of the CDs released each year flop--at great expense to the companies, not the artists. It's an industry, the executives say, in which even unknown acts are treated like royalty, receiving millions of dollars in advances per project as their labels struggle to transform them into global stars.

To bolster their point, executives from Vivendi Universal, AOL Time Warner, Sony, Bertelsmann and EMI Group provided The Times access to internal budgets and cost-analysis data for dozens of recording projects, from marquee stars to failed unknowns. The information was disclosed on condition that no specific artist would be named in this article. Executives for the companies agreed to be interviewed on the condition that they would not be identified.

The documents disclose the following:

* Only one of 10 acts ever turns a profit.

* It costs about $2 to manufacture and distribute a CD, but marketing costs can run from $3 per hit CD to more than $10 for failed projects.

* Successful acts thwart the existing contract system by refusing to deliver follow-up albums until they extract additional advances.

"You might want to ask yourself why it is that most recording stars that have the opportunity to exit the major label system typically re-sign with a major label," said Hilary Rosen, president of the Recording Industry Assn. of America, the Washington trade group that represents the nation's largest music companies. "There is a very simple reason: Record companies know how to market and promote records to mass audiences. And they take huge financial risks that help advance artists' careers--risks that few artists are willing to take on their own." But rock stars such as Love and Don Henley say the execs can do a better job and treat artists more fairly in the process.

They and 100 other acts in the Recording Artists Coalition have pledged to launch a trade group or a union to challenge the industry tradition of long-term contracts that keep acts tied up for years longer than is legal in other industries, including film and sports. Under the standard contract, artists are prevented from owning their original music and, after attaining

success, must repay companies for financing their recordings, videos, retail placement and tour support.

The standard contracts also allow companies to deduct fees for a variety of promotional expenses and to pay artists reduced royalty rates for albums sold overseas and through record clubs. "Record companies get away with their sloppy and obsolete system of accounting," said Love. "They are terrified of having their practices exposed. "The state of California and the stockholders need to know that they're missing out on billions in revenues and thousands of jobs because of this unwillingness to stop the excess and stupidity of the old-fashioned system," the singer said.

But to hear the corporations tell it, contemporary artists have little to complain about. Even those whose contracts are severed, executives contend, earn the opportunity to pursue their creative dreams on the company's dime. Failed unknowns walk away debt-free, no matter how many millions of dollars in losses they leave behind. And the artists who produce hits, executives say, typically renegotiate for even larger advances and frequently parlay their musical fame into other financial opportunities. Superstars can earn millions of dollars from concerts, commercial endorsements, merchandising, music publishing and acting deals--none of which they share with their labels. Nonetheless, record company executives are reluctant to publicly challenge the artists. And for good reason, Rosen said. "It's their job to promote artists, not attack them," she said. "They see no upside in alienating their own artists, even when they're feeling abused. No act wants to work with a company that

21

bad-mouths artists."

It's true, companies acknowledge, that years ago artists were not always compensated fairly. The industry's history is rife with tales of great musicians who signed away their rights for a pittance and died broke. It wasn't uncommon during the 1950s and '60s for artists such as Motown singer Mary Wells and blues act Jimmy Reed to suffer at the hands of unscrupulous managers, lawyers, concert promoters and independent labels who once dominated pop music.

But these days, executives say, the $40-billion industry, which throws off an estimated $3.5 billion in annual operating profit, is run by public corporations that pay artists fair royalties commensurate with the risk each party takes. Even the most obscure acts, they say, now enter the business represented by competent attorneys who negotiate fair deals. And artists who do not want to sign a major label contract always have the option of putting out their own recordings.

The five music conglomerates spend billions of dollars each year to keep their global star-making machines intact. The industry employs about 50,000 people, and the price of signing talent, producing videos and promoting records continues to skyrocket, squeezing margins in a business already threatened by Internet piracy. "If this was an industry showing Microsoft-like profits, the artists might have an easier battle ahead of them," said Michael Nathanson, a media analyst at investment firm Sanford C. Bernstein & Co. "But music margins are under serious pressure, growth is nearly negative and everybody's already scrambling to cut jobs. The business is a mess."

Statistics tabulated by SoundScan, an independent research firm that monitors U.S. record sales, confirm the industry's predicament. Of the 6,188 albums released last year, only 50 sold more than a million copies. Sixty-five sold 500,000 units and 356 sold 100,000 or more. In other words, more than 90% of last year's releases flopped. Generally, a major-label album needs to sell about 400,000 copies to reach

22

profitability.

"People who don't understand the business just look at what makes it to the top of the chart," said SoundScan CEO Mike Shalett. "They fail to appreciate what it takes cost-wise to get there. "Companies invest enormous amounts of capital trying to make hit records. It's like searching for a needle in a haystack." Few artists concern themselves with the financial intricacies of record-making. Indeed, most musicians enter the business with nothing more than a demo and a desire to become famous. Once an act begins to exhibit commercial potential, however, it usually doesn't take long to rustle up a deal.

The drill, executives say, goes like this: After the artist solicits an offer from one label, his or her attorney usually contacts competitors in an effort to drive up the signing price. A bidding war can ensue and, by the time it's over, the act normally walks away with a check for about $750,000 to cover recording costs and living expenses. (*That's for pop and urban acts. Rock and country acts are often paid less.*) All five major labels provided The Times with lists of their latest failed acts to support their contention that artists are often the only ones making money on these projects.

In the case of one unknown act that received a $750,000 advance, the money was allocated to cover the cost of recording its first album and to provide the group with about $250,000 to live on, after deducting legal and management fees. The contract required the singers to repay the $750,000 and all other advances from future sales, assuming the album did well, before receiving any royalties. After the artists turned in the finished studio recording, the company invested an additional $2.8 million to roll out a marketing campaign to reach retail stores, radio, musical networks MTV and Black Entertainment Television, which play crucial roles in stimulating music sales. A big chunk of that money, approximately $800,000, went to produce two videos, neither of which ended up getting much airplay on cable music shows. Another $800,000 was set aside for independent promoters to pitch the first two singles to radio programmers. Neither single got much play before being axed from broadcast playlists.

Over the course of a six-month campaign, the company spent an additional $1.2 million for retail product placement, tour support, photo shoots, advertising and radio and TV show appearances to boost the CD. Despite the effort, the album sold only about 100,000 copies and the label decided to drop the act. The company lost more than $2.7 million on the project. The artists walked away debt-free. If a company decides to risk a follow-up on a failed act,

the meter starts running again. Either way, the corporation eats the loss. But the music companies get no sympathy from attorney Jay Cooper, whose clients include Recording Artist Coalition co-founder Sheryl Crow. "These companies are run by intelligent, well-paid executives who have no one to blame but themselves that the industry's failure rate is so high," Cooper said.

Cooper and other critics contend that the record labels should be more discriminating when signing artists and stop wasting so much money on videos, retail positioning and independent promotion. If executives ran their labels more efficiently, critics say, they could afford to pay better royalties to the artists who succeed, instead of forcing them to offset the losses of so many failures.

Why, critics ask, does Wall Street bother with a business that doles out millions of dollars each year in salaries and bonuses to executives who fail so frequently? The record companies respond that music is not a commodity and that public taste is not easy to discern. Executives who deliver the hits, companies say, are entitled to the big bucks they earn. And to hear them tell it, artists aren't always so altruistic either. Each of the major labels privately shared horror stories involving a number of successful newcomers who dominated the pop charts last year. Two of those acts racked up more than $18 million each in marketing expenses on their first albums. One singer charged the company $2 million just to make a video. Another billed the label $250,000 to film a 15-second video sequence. Several entertainers billed their labels more than $20,000 each for hair and makeup "glam squad" fees every time they appeared on TV.

Overnight sensations aren't shy either about using their newfound leverage to strong-arm labels for additional money not covered under their contracts. "About six seconds before they go back into the studio to record the follow-up, you get the gun to your head," said one label chief. "We call it the second-album hold-up. They want bigger advances. They want better royalties. The risk escalates exponentially." One pop

act, whose debut album sold 7 million copies, demanded a $13-million advance before returning to the studio. Another act, whose debut album sold 4 million units, refused to deliver a follow-up until it received a $4-million advance and a beefed-up royalty. The band pocketed the money and the album bombed.

Executives say the success rate for follow-up albums by blockbuster bands is no better than for debut acts. "The problem is almost nobody has more than a three-album shelf life in this fickle market," said one executive. To make matters worse, superstars are having a tough time delivering hits. Companies say they are still smarting from a spate of expensive deals negotiated during the middle and late 1990s. The concept behind such deals is that career acts create a body of work that will sell for a long time. Indeed, the value of a record company hinges primarily on the size and quality of its catalog. That's why labels are so adamant about owning the master recordings of the acts they sign to long-term deals. But in a business threatened by encroaching Internet piracy, companies have watched catalog sales slip from about 50% to 38% over the last decade.

In one recent case, a label signed a $25-million, three-album pact with a superstar act that broke up shortly after delivering one CD. That CD sold fewer than 300,000 copies. Another label signed a $30-million, three-album deal with a star who took four years to

25

deliver his first recording, which ended up selling fewer than 500,000 copies. Four of the five music conglomerates are saddled with similar money-losing propositions. "You know, sometimes running a record company feels like working in the emergency room of a hospital or a cancer ward," said one executive. "The odds are so severely stacked against you. No matter how hard you try, in the end you know from experience that the vast majority won't make it. "Every now and then you get lucky. It's not as easy as it looks."

Related articles on the economics of the record industry are available at: http://www.latimes.com/recordbiz

CHAPTER 2

Music Production

MUSIC PRODUCTION
(Pre and Post Production)

Music Production is the very key to having a successful album, not to mention it has heavy implications in regard to public buy in, radio support, trade reviews, as well as show or touring support. Major labels usually spend for the production of an album a minimum of $100,000. As an independent label you want to be able to have high-quality production at minimum costs, so that you will be able to place most of your budgets into the promotion campaign. Keys to achieving that goal would be in the pre-production arena. Having a music workstation would cut down tremendously the costs accrued in the recording studio. Most music workstations have 16 tracks of recording and an unlimited amount of layering, along with mix-down and effects. A good producer can produce an entire album on a music workstation and then go into a recording studio with the workstation and single out each individual track to the system the recording studio is using. This will save you money and time in the long run, along with diminishing pressures while you are creating each song. An ideal studio would be one that has Protools or a similar software program, capable of recording each track and individually manipulating them through its excellent editing effects. A good engineer who is knowledgeable in the utilization of such production software programs will have a major impact on the achievement of quality in the recording process, not to mention, he or she will be able to move very quickly throughout the recording sessions, again cutting down on your cost factor. Many studios are equipped with such production aides, but only the producers or engineers truly versed in their use will be able to garner all that the programs have to offer and apply it to the production of your project.

Once the album is recorded, you will have to deal with the mix-down, which in itself is probably the most important part of the recording. What I have found to be easiest in regards to the mix-down is having the entire project recorded at the same studio, whereby making the mix-down easy since all the recording levels are the same. A good rule of thumb, is to have a (new) engineer who has fresh ears to the project, who will be an asset by having new ideas and a fresh perspective to add to the quality and sound of the project. This is so very critical, everyone deeply involved in the recording process can easily loose perspective by the end of the process making the final stages of production very tedious and counter-productive. Lastly, the Mastering, yes this too is critical, you would be surprised how many projects slip through without being mastered. Mastering takes the project to a whole new level and can quite often be the lynch pin to achieving quality in the studio; it is without a doubt what ice-cream is to apple pie. The good news is, now there are mastering programs that can match any high-quality recorded album and duplicate it graphically in terms of levels, pitches, equalization, etc. This could be the one thing that could get you that airplay, product placement or customer buy-in that you are seeking. Commercial regular rotation radio has very high requisite standards with respect to production quality. Otherwise radio playable tracks are frequently refused airplay as a result of poor production.

Indeed this book is primarily about music distribution, but it would be remiss to not devote text to the creative processes that are at the foundation of every music product release.

MUSIC VIDEO PRE AND POST PRODUCTION

The first step in the entire process of Music Video Production is to determine if the production of the music video is feasible. Therefore a feasibility study should be conducted. Will you be able to sell enough units to cover your production expenses and make a profit? Yes, music videos can be attributable for up to

20% of album sales. However, if your budgets are limited and there is no activity on album sales, it cannot be cost justified. Things to examine are the budgets, approval process, stylistic approach, time frame, and understanding the entire production process.

BUDGET

Budget is ALWAYS a major factor when considering whether to produce media content. However, it is practically impossible for a Producer or Production Company to quote a dollar figure for your production without first knowing some specific information. A good Producer will help you to figure this out in a step-by-step process by asking a series of questions which will help you to flesh out your idea and make it more concrete. This is a good way to find out what you need to find out before you proceed with spending a lot of money.

The Producer's job is to "manage" the production by balancing the client's vision, directives, time frame and budget into cohesiveness while meeting their goals. Music Video Production can start at $2,000 for (video) and $9,000 for (film) and go into the millions. Of course 35mm film is the way to go, it can be as low as $9,000 for a basic video at (1) location. You can also shoot in 16mm or super 16mm film cutting down the costs as well. What is interesting is you could save hundreds of dollars by shooting on super 16mm film, and by shooting medium and close-up cameos on the artist, with great lighting in the studio, it literally could pass for 35mm film production, if done correctly. Of course this is the Producer's job to help you understand the cost implications of each decision you make about your project. The clearer you can be about the details of your project, the closer you are to an answer for... "How much is this going to cost?"

APPROVAL PROCESS

It is important to have a limited amount of people involved in the approval process, maintaining focus and centralized control of the project. Getting feedback on the project is good with a team of people, however, only the people working directly on the project will have a more realistic approach on decision making.

STYLISTIC APPROACH

Stylistic approach simply refers to the 'look' and 'style' of your project. What kind of music video do you want? Special effects? Cameos only? Perhaps 2-3 outdoor locations? A scene shot in Mid-Manhattan or shot in the studio with stock film of Mid-Manhattan in background? Certain styles fit better with different types of projects and the music also can change the outlook of the video. When considering these styles, bear in mind your audience. What would be appropriate for them? These decisions are up to you and your video team. You want to balance creativity with effective communication of your message. Pre-production is the key to a successful music video. You will need to plan out all the necessary steps involved, along with the approach, realistic budgets, and keeping the project within the time frame.

TIME FRAME

Just as important as the budget is a clear understanding of the time frame needed to create a project. In many cases, you will be working toward a specific deadline for the completion of your video. Factor in the time it will take to shoot the video, special effects, animation, editing, feedback and the final editing phase. A good producer with a lot of experience can save you a lot of money and time by dealing efficiently with problems that he or she has encountered on previous shoots. Just by incorporating new ideas for your project, the producer can assist in making it realistic and feasible. Sometimes, you will come to the hard realization that you aren't able to do your planned video due to a lack of adequate budget or timeframe. This can be more painful to learn after you've begun your project and been forced to ask for more time and money.

UNDERSTANDING THE ENTIRE PRODUCTION PROCESS

The production process typically breaks down into four phases:
• Pre-Production
• Production
• Post-Production
• Distribution

In the Pre-Production Phase representatives of the client and the producer meet to identify and finalize all program elements. Elements such as: research and scripting needs, a stylistic "look" for the program, the need for actors and/or sets, the selection of those people and locations to appear in the video, identifying special graphical elements such as animation or photo-animation, determining the need for narration and music, any travel needs, and overall program length. Once these issues have been clarified, the producer can then develop an itemized Production Budget and Project Timeline to be submitted to the client for approval.

At this point many different things can happen, such as acceptance of the proposal and progressing to the signing of a contract, a revision of the budget and timeline, a delay of the project to wait for additional funding, or rejection of the proposal outright. Once a proposal is accepted by the client, a Production Schedule is created in consultation with many people. This will translate all of the elements in the desired final program into days of production. Most projects require 2-4 days of production, but of course, there are always exceptions.

The Production Phase is the actual filming of the project segments over a period of days. This can be done locally or on location in another city, in a studio, office or virtually anywhere. This will occur with a selected video crew and with varying types of equipment. The specific crew and equipment needs, and the amount of days required for videotaping will have been determined during the pre-production phase. The client should be present for some if not all of the Production Phase in case any last minute questions or issues arise. This is also the phase where the majority of the project budget is spent. Once this phase is completed, there are still many more steps required to shape the raw footage into the final product.

In The Post-Production Phase all of your footage is copied, edited and 'shaped' into its final form in a series of stages which may take several weeks. You will have a choice whether to edit your tape in an Analog video suite or a Digital Suite.
Steps involved would include:
• Copy your original footage to protect it, and then work with those copies until the final edit stage. If something goes wrong and you accidentally destroy a tape copy – no problem! You can always make a new copy from the original footage.
• Log your footage and transcribe any interviews you might have. This will inform you of exactly everything you have and where it is.
• The rough edit process – This is usually the longest single phase of assembling your Program. It may take a few days, weeks or even a few months.
• Selecting Narration, Music, Graphics, Transitions, Titles, Credits, Animation. These can lend your program a professional polish.
• Copying your final Program Edit – Just in case you lose it, anything can happen, so have an extra copy.

MVPA
How do you find great music video production companies? Well you could start with the MVPA (Music Video Production Association) a non-profit trade organization that has production companies under membership. Their work is of undeniable high quality, yet they are open for any budget negotiations, while keeping the project creative. The MVPA is a non-profit trade organization created to address the mutual concerns of its members in today's highly competitive, ever changing music video industry. Its membership includes music video production and post-production companies, as well as individual editors, directors,
32

producers, cinematographers, choreographers, script supervisors, computer animators and make-up artists, to name a few. Their associate membership includes suppliers and service providers. The MVPA, which maintains chapters in Los Angeles and New York, represents the people responsible for the vast majority of the music videos produced in the world today.

The purpose of the MVPA is to promote and uphold the highest professional production standards, to provide an arena to share ideas and to educate members about the latest developments in the music video industry. The MVPA also provides a forum through which discussions of mutual concern can occur between production companies, record labels, crews, suppliers and all interested parties.

Widely recognized as the official organization representing music video production companies, the MVPA offers its members, cutting-edge information through its quarterly newsletter; up-to-date production and record company mailing lists; meetings with committees and special forums to discuss pressing issues. The MVPA Web site is an expanding source for production information and tools that aid production professionals. With industry-wide nominations and membership voting, the MVPA Annual Awards, provides the only awards forum that recognizes the technical and creative artisans of music video production. The awards are presented at a gala event held in Los Angeles. The Artfest is an event that showcases a variety of artwork by music video directors. The Director's Cuts Film Festival is a bi-coastal event that provides an opportunity for music video directors to showcase their short films and experimental pieces to agencies and feature film representatives. In addition, the MVPA hosts educational seminars on areas such as pre and post production techniques, special effects, and workshops on camera and film stock.

CHAPTER 3

Manufacturing Processes, Systems & Product Platforms

MANUFACTURING PROCESS

It always surprises me when companies or artists just choose any manufacturer without shopping around, especially when you consider how such a lack of diligence can affect your bottom line. When focusing on possible higher net profits from album sales, manufacturing cost factors will weigh heavily in this regard. First of all, you as an independent label, will only receive $7.00 to $8.00 gross on the full-length album from your distributor. $8.00 is only if you have a major act or the artist is moving a decent amount of units via retail sell-through, so lets say we are only dealing with the $7.00 gross.

If you are paying $2.00 to $2.50 per unit (CD) for manufacturing, you are now down to $4.50 on your way from gross to net, we haven't even touched on artist royalties, radio and retail promotions, music production or any other aspect or accrued expense that has to be recouped on the road to net. Now you can see the importance of having a good manufacturing company who can give you a lower rate, and at the same time, fast turnaround and a high-quality product. Controlling such costs is crucial to the profitability of any indie release. The goal is to find a manufacturing company capable of extending to you a volume rate-base, based on the total volume of manufacturing you give them in a fiscal year. The smart thing to do is to form a collective with a few artists or independent labels and group your manufacturing patronage under one account. This way you should benefit from the lower rates afforded those with volume account status. It is a generalization, but there are discounts in volume. Now you are talking around .80 to .90 based on volume and for a run of 2500 CDs manufactured. The money saved is money earned which will reflect directly on your net profits.

PRODUCT PLATFORMS

This is a term used for any medium or format used to host music, examples are: CD, CDR, Cassettes, Vinyl, DAT, Mini-disc. Currently Cassettes are fading away in the US market, and believe it or not distributors are refusing to distribute cassettes, so the primary product platform you should focus on are CDs. You will still need to press vinyl for the benefit of Club and Radio DJ's who prefer wax to CD. This is very important in terms of club and radio promotion, mix-shows, record pools, etc. This is another avenue to garner exposure, not to mention add support to your campaign.

In an article released in August, 2002 written by renown radio promotions professional and Music Industry veteran Bryan Farrish of Bryan Farrish Radio Promotions, Farrish speaks directly to the resurgence of vinyl as a product platform. Particularly with respect to his area of overwhelming expertise, radio promotion. From his article series Airplay 101, here is that article.

Using Vinyl for Airplay -Bryan Farrish

Most people reading this won't know this, but vinyl (or "wax") is actually growing in popularity. And radio, although it never totally dropped using vinyl, is now increasing its use of wax in particular formats. You may have even heard the scratches purposely put on some urban or pop recordings to simulate real vinyl.

You may have guessed that hip hop and rap are the prime users of vinyl. While this is true, pop, hot AC, electronic, ambient, and even some mainstream-AC or country dance "re-mixes" can make use of vinyl. The main indicator of the need of vinyl is how much potential there is for dance club play of the club remix.

Starting with college radio, if you are doing hip hop or rap, then vinyl is nice but not mandatory. Projects with vinyl will do a lot better, but it's still possible to get most-added (and then chart) on CMJ without ever pressing wax. Same for electronica (i.e., "RPM"). But due to the large number of college stations, it is understandable that not all projects will have the budget for wax.

Commercial mix-show, however, requires vinyl, period. These guys are your main leads into club play and record pools, and indeed, they are sometimes the very same people who mix the clubs (or run the pools) anyway. You can almost do mix-shows without even having CDs, but don't try it... you'll be sacrificing some airplay. This applies to any genre that can spin in a mix-show.

With commercial regular rotation, the use of wax gets back to how much mix-show is being pushed at the same time. If mix is definitely part of it, they you have to do wax. But there is also a splash factor with wax, which becomes important, and it ties into the other standard marketing items like trade support. When you have wax, you are taken much more seriously, even though for regular rotation the stations are just going to dump the CD onto their hard drive.

So for a basic regular rotation push, you can use just CD; for a good push you must use CD and wax; for a serious push you must push wax and CD to both regular rotation and mix-show (and for a heavy-duty push, you have to work regular rotation separate from mix, and you have to service and work each mix-show guy separately... usually at their homes and on their cells.)

It should be noted that mix-shows are not the same as record pools. Record pools are for club servicing only; they do not cross over to radio mix-show.

QUANTITY: For college, if you only do one piece of wax per station, you'll need at least 200 to 300 wax (and CDs) for the basic reporting panel of CMJ. If you want to hit each DJ with a separate piece, you'll need more like 500.

For mix-show, if you are only servicing the mixers (and not the PD/MD) and if you are only giving one piece per person, you'll need about 600 pieces for the basic 300 stations that have active mix-shows which report to the trades (there are more, but they don't report.) If you want to include the PD/MD, that's an extra 2 per commercial station, or about an extra 300. Finally, if you are going to be giving the mixers copies for them to give to the clubs, you'll need an extra 300 to 600. Keep in mind when you are servicing wax, you need to send it (with CDs) in a priority box. Otherwise it may get delayed 2 to 3 weeks.

• **Bryan Farrish Radio Promotions – "Airplay 101"** / airplay-articles@radio-media.com / **www.radio-media.com**

CHAPTER 4

Distribution Companies

DISTRIBUTION PLATFORMS

The easiest and most comprehensive way to break down the distribution platform is to first fully understand the job of a distributor; which in short, is to transfer product from the record label to the retail outlet, serving as the conduit to point of sale (P.O.S.). There are several types of distribution companies capable of handling the job, some are wholly owned divisions of established record labels, others are independent operations. Here are the recognized categories of distribution firms: Major Label Distributors are the largest and dominate the distribution arena, mainly distributing major label products and are directly affiliated with the major labels serving in the capacity of exclusive fulfillment for their affiliated major label. There are (5) major label distributors: BMG, EMI, UNI, SONY and WEA. They all have tremendous warehouse facilities, capable of distributing their product within a 24-period into all major retail outlets, one-stops and rack jobbers throughout the US. They are for the most part, very well resourced and their catalogs very well represented to retail Buyers at the corporate levels for nationwide buy-in and placement. These major distribution firms are additionally financially resourced to support any given project or title under distribution. The subsidiaries and partners they distribute for are exemplary of the giants of the Music Industry; for example: BMG distributes Arista, RCA, Windham Hill Records, BadBoy Entertainment, and J-Records titles; EMI distributes EMI, Capitol, and Virgin titles; UNI distributes Universal, MCA, Polygram, Geffen, A&M, Mercury and Motown titles; Sony distributes Sony, Columbia and Epic titles; while, WEA distributes Warner Bros., Elektra, Atlantic and Asylum titles.

(MAJOR) INDEPENDENT DISTRIBUTORS

Distribution has changed within the last few years, substantially, which is the reason for the term (Major) independent distribution companies, encompassing those companies that have the capability to place product in most or all major music retail chain outlets and one-stops within a 24-hr period. These distributors are also fully-staffed with their own marketing, accounting, advertising, sales, shipping and receiving departments, housing products in their warehouse facilities, some equaling the size of the major distribution companies' facilities. They are also capable of manufacturing product when needed using their own financial reserves or credit lines and not the labels, along with fronting retail advertising costs on projects that have decent sales activity. Examples of (Major) Independent Distributors would be: Koch Intl, ADA, Bayside Entertainment Distribution, Red, and Navarre. Obtaining distribution through a major independent firm is difficult. Many of their operational business models are based on volume, therefore they are selective about who they sign. Typically they look to sign labels that have multiple titles, a solid roster with perhaps 4 to 6 strong titles with good marketing push behind them giving strong reason to believe that significant sales potential exist. Many times with these firms, you will need sales history verifiable through SoundScan to obtain the coveted distribution services. It is not likely that these firms will grant distribution to an independent label with only 1 or 2 projects or an individual artist unless the projects have clear and impressive sales history.

INDEPENDENT DISTRIBUTORS

These distributors vary in size and cover US national distribution as well as regional distribution. Most of these distributors specialize in specific genres of music choosing to operate within a niche market. Most independent labels are distributed by the independent distribution companies, which themselves, usually have other relationships, affiliations or distribution contracts with other distributors and one-stops creating a sort of daisy chain network or pipeline of distribution. What is interesting is that Major labels go through these independent distributors as well, since they have great relationships with specialty retailers and have "niche" audiences. These operations also have specialized offices covering regional areas of the US, adding to the support of their targeted areas of distribution. It is true that with these firms you are more likely to benefit from aggressive retail promotion. With far fewer titles in their catalogs, it behooves these firms to aggressively seek product placement at retail POS; each title must sell through to some degree for the business model to work. An additional benefit of the smaller catalog is that your title is more likely to receive greater attention as it will not simply be one of possibly hundreds under distribution. Independent distribution can be a tremendous stepping stone for indie releases, garnering the requisite sales history perhaps regionally to move up to a major independent firm. Depending on the "daisy chain-like" network of your independent distributor, you may find their reach to be sufficient, such that you never out grow their capacity to place your product. You must note that dealing with an independent distributor may cut into your margin a bit more than direct distribution. These firms are essentially middle men in the supply chain. They are granting you distribution via their proprietary affiliation, usually with a major independent distributor. The larger affiliate is returning to the independent a gross from retail minus their fee and then the independent distributor is deducting their fee or percentage in addition to that; all prior to you receiving your disbursement. An additional point is that related aspects and processes of distribution, such as returns, recalls and payment disbursement may take longer because the process must administratively run through 2 companies. All in all, for the indie label, independent distribution is the answer, it represents a distribution solution that is within your grasp.

ONESTOP DISTRIBUTORS
One-stops are regional operations that obtain product from Major labels and independent distributors. They are able to sell in smaller quantities to the mom and pop stores and specialty stores, while they are still capable of buying in large quantities from major and independent distributors. The one-stop distributor can

39

also fill back-orders for the major record chains. Examples of One-stops: Southwest Wholesale, Music Network, Arrow, Central South Wholesale and Super Discount. From the retail perspective, one-stops provide inventory with minimal restrictions on buying for smaller independent, regional chain or singular outlets. These retailers can not and do not need to purchase large numbers of units per title. One-stops afford these retailers the ability to purchase even 1 or 2 units of a particular title for their small operations. More and more independent labels and individual artist are seeking and obtaining direct distribution with one-stops local to their home market. This is a growing and very wise trend. Typically the mom & pop retailers in their backyard are buying direct from these one-stops, stores that are receiving direct promotional attention from the independent label or artist. If the product is readily available through the retailer's usual supplier, and they can physically see promotional activities being conducted in their very town or market, they are more apt to purchase the units and you are more likely to see sell through at these outlets. Now you are building a sales history for your release. Since the one-stops are dealing directly to retail you are likely to be maximizing your per unit profits. Some larger one-stops offer far greater than basic regional distribution and place product in larger retail chains as well.

RACK JOBBERS

Rack Jobbers sell audio recordings in the non-traditional music retail stores. Stores such as K-Mart, Walmart lease shelve space to, and are serviced by the Rack Jobber. A customer walking into a large retail store cannot know just by looking around whether that music product selling area is a department of the store, whether it is space leased to an outside firm, or whether it is serviced by a jobber who supplies the racks and bins. Chances are, a rack jobber is servicing that record selling operation. Jobbers work out various kinds of contracts with the store that supplies the retail space. Among the most common:

1. The jobber rents space for racks and bins from the retailer for a flat monthly fee. The jobber offers complete servicing of the area and retains all the money collected from sales.

2. The jobber pays the host store a percentage of sales.

3. The jobber and store management work out a minimum lease fee, then if sales exceed an agreed-upon figure in any given month, the jobber pays the store a percentage of the overage.

Retailers like record racks on their premises because they can often make more profit per square foot of floor space from this kind of merchandise than they can from other lines. Merchants also benefit from increased shopper traffic generated by the high volume of music product buyers. Rack jobbers acquire such leases or arrangements by detailing to the retailer that they can "turn" or derive profit from even the smallest area of floor space. Retailers don't operate out of large commercial spaces to provide more room for their customers, they do so because greater floor space provides the opportunity to house larger inventories which if carefully selected, can lead to greater gross revenues.

When rack jobbing of records was in its early stages (*late 1950s, early 1960s*), jobbers were content to lease small areas near checkout stands. These tiny displays had space to accommodate a very limited variety of records. Jobbers tended to display just the current super-hits and only some of them. The balance of the limited space was given to cutouts (*overstock sale products*). This limitation of space helped foster the hit records syndrome: Only the hits were made available on the racks. Newer artists or lesser known records never got a chance to be seen or heard.

Rack jobbers continue these small operations in a variety of locations. But today some installations rival in size the conventional record stores. When a rack jobber sets up a large number of racks and bins, the jobber needs clerks to assist customers and restock supplies daily. Where a rack setup of this size is in operation, it is practically indistinguishable from a "leased department." When a jobber leases enough space for this kind of operation, the jobber has a major commitment of capital and will probably have a dedicated checkout counter and handle money separately. Leased departments are common in department stores and discount chains. Large retailers can demand hefty lease payments from the record merchant/jobber and, at the same time, are spared all responsibility of running the record sales department.

Large retailers and chains, observing the success on their premises of these record sales operations, will, from time to time, decide to take over the same space, install their own record department management, then pocket the percentage formerly kept by the rack jobber. Rack jobbers try to anticipate this kind of temptation by offering the store trouble-free, profitable operations, sparing retailers the problem' of trying to run a kind of retailing they do not really understand.

Individuals who started out as rack jobbers or distributors are now also heavily involved in operating "stand-alone" retail outlets. The lines between record distribution, jobbing, and retailing are now blurred; some of the most successful merchants operate in all three areas. This blending of record selling operations was originally accelerated by the need of merchants to buy products at ever-higher discounts through volume purchasing. The largest Rack jobbers of music product in the US are Handleman Corp. (*servicing K-Mart*) and Anderson Merchandisers (*servicing Wal-Mart*).

RETAIL CHAIN STORES
As music software retailing becomes bigger, the smaller entrepreneur becomes easy prey. The growth of record chain operations results in pressures already cited. To make a profit, the merchants must find ever new ways to buy cheaper, and the mass merchandiser is certainly in a better position to do this than mom and pop. Another advantage is that chain store advertising is far more cost-effective than a mom-and-pop campaign-which can rarely include an important medium like TV. Chain store operators provide an additional advantage to their component units. When one store overbuys and gets stuck with inventory, it can often shift some of this product to another unit in the chain that may have run short. Chain store members help each other balance their inventories. The largest Retail Chain is Best Buy which now owns

Musicland, and SamGoody. Others are Transworld-which is FYE (For Your Entertainment) and Camelot Music, Tower, Borders, Virgin Mega, and Wherehouse. The overwhelming obvious benefit to obtaining placement for your release at major retail is that this is where enormous volume sell through can occur; major retail moves units. Where the mom & pops outlets are buying-in regionally perhaps, 2 to 5 units in each of a handful of outlets, major retail can potentially buy-in 1 to 3 thousand units regionally and possibly as much as 10 to 25 thousand units per purchase order for national placement if they feel it is warranted due to projected sell through. Such activity will likely require, minimally, a major independent distributor or at least an independent distributor with a broad network and an affiliation with a major independent distributor.

CHAPTER 5

Distribution Processes

RECORD DISTRIBUTION
If initial promotional and marketing efforts are even moderately successful in generating a buzz, consumer interest, in a new music release, the label must find a way to get the product to potential consumers. This must be done wherever they may be, at the right time and in sufficient quantities to not only satisfy that current demand, but also to meet projected demand based on anticipated continued promotional advances in given markets. This is a very difficult thing to do with precise timing and accuracy, for the market is unpredictable and widely dispersed. After 50 years of trial and error, even major labels are still trying to figure out a more efficient distribution system. As for small labels, the lack of effective distribution has caused many to fail in the marketplace. After all, the inability to achieve product placement at POS, and more specifically, in particular markets where there exist a demand or consumer interest, will take the wind from the sails of any new music product release.

Until about mid-century, only a handful of companies were in the recording business. Each had its own procedure for delivering its products to consumers. With the rapid proliferation of labels in the 1950s, newcomers to the market often lacked an understanding of the essential need for a national network of distributors to get their products to retail outlets. Smaller labels would seek larger ones to distribute their records. Other new labels contracted the services of the growing number of independent distributors that were setting up operations in most markets. In the years since, some regional independent distributors have formed national distribution networks. Many of the distribution problems and inefficiencies that have troubled the industry since the 1920s remain focal points today.

Record retailing has been plagued by price wars among merchants, which have had a direct and culminating effect upon the distributors. Merchants fighting to remain afloat amidst irrational retail pricing competition appeal to their distributors for deeper discounts to help them survive the competition. Distributors can respond to these appeals most often when they can sell at high volume. For you economics majors, that's "volume economics"; acceptance or realization of a lessor margin with the expectation of profiting more substantially overall by moving greater volume. But when a merchant becomes too aggressive, buying-in, and becomes over burdened with expensive, stagnant inventory, the distributor will soon hear a plea for lenient "return privileges".

Distributors try to strike a balance between overselling their accounts or offering an undersupply. With the former, both parties suffer the inconvenience and expense of returns; only the shipping industry, and possibly the paper industry, profits with returns. But when a distributor's customers buy too conservatively and a recording hits suddenly, both parties miss out on sales when the merchandise is not available to the buying public. Consumer interest can be fleeting, the window of opportunity to profit from promotionally generated consumer demand can close rapidly. Smart distributors try to guide retailers in their buying so as to minimize returns, because when merchandise flows in the wrong direction, everyone gets hurt and the truth is that the title in question may not get a second chance, at least not in that particular market.

RETURNS
Distributors and sales personnel can often pressure dealers to buy more stock than they believe they can move as a result of internal or external pressures to move particular blocks of inventory or just inventory in general. This pressure will manifest various forms, generally in some way at least momentarily attractive to the merchant. Record companies or distributors will often offer merchants liberal merchandise return privileges or discount on volume purchase orders, any number of methods to entice the retailer to buy-in

45

heavier than perhaps they had initially planned. In the past, practically all records and tapes in this country were sold on consignment; if you can't sell the merchandise, return it for full credit. In the 1980s, most labels and distributors tightened 19their return policies. The practice now is often one that requires the merchant to return the stock within a predetermined time limit and to return only a pre-stated percentage of the total units originally ordered. Labels' return policies accelerated the demise of vinyl products, especially singles. When record companies disallowed the return of vinyl 45s, many retailers were unwilling or unable to continue stocking them. Return policies themselves have become competitive aspects of distribution. They are very carefully stipulated and closely reviewed line items within distribution Vendor Agreements, often being one of the more heavily weighted factors in deciding which firm to go with. A distributor with extreme, punitive and restrictive return policies may have greater difficulty persuading retail to buy from them, particularly independent music product. This is because with such stringent return policies, sell through becomes even more critical and independent releases tend to have far fewer promotional dollars behind them therefore making sell through far from guaranteed. Conversely, a distributor with very liberal return policies may find itself being taken advantage of in the wholesale marketplace.

PRICING

In order to get a distributor to carry your product, you'll have to convince them that your records are going to sell through or at least have the potential to do so. If you don't have prior sales history to speak of for the title, you must demonstrate the potential of the release, even if just in a particular market or region. This means providing them with at least college radio playlists and airplay confirmation, good reviews, proposed advertisement schedules for radio and print, current touring / performance schedules and additional current or proposed promotional efforts. Offering all of this to them to evidence potential will have an even greater impact if it is primarily relegated to one

46

particular market or region.

If a distributor agrees to stock your record they will ask for a wholesale price per unit, CD. You will be hard pressed to find a distributor that will buy vinyl from an independent band, but for full-length cassettes the ballpark price is between $4.50 and $5.50. For full length CDs it's between $7.00 and $8.50. EPs (*three to six songs*) and extended length releases are slightly less and more, respectively. This is not the price at which retail buy-in will occur, it is the dollar return the distributor gives you. Based on these rather standard dollar return figures, the distributor will sell your product to retail for about $9.49 to $10.89 per unit for a full length CD and roughly $6.00 to $7.50 for a full length cassette. Retail will be informed of the SRP or suggested retail price for your product but are actually free to price it as they see fit. Both the retail buy-in rate as well as your dollar return rate are fixed (*flat rate*) and will not fluctuate based on anything retail chooses to do with respect to pricing. The system works, you need not worry about retail trying to maximize profits by marking your product at outrageously high prices therefore hindering sales. The system works because everyone in it is operating toward but one objective, to sell units.

DISTRIBUTION PAYMENT TERMS

Distributors are generally looking to get the longest possible terms on which to pay out on a disbursement schedule. The disbursement schedule is the aspect you eagerly await. It is the product, or end result of retail sell-through and the end of the distribution cycle. First, you advance the distributor "X" number of units of your release, (*get them to pay the freight or designate the shipping company they use*). Second, you invoice them on the units advanced, (*send them a bill*). Depending on the terms you agree to, they are obligated to pay you within either 30, 45, 60, 90 or 120 days from the date of the invoice. As the label, you want to negotiate the shortest terms possible. As an Indie, cash flow is critical and capital reserve is king. The sooner you are able to realize the fiscal return from sell-through, the sooner you are able to allocate additional dollars back into your project; dollars you will no doubt require to press more units and keep the promotional wheel turning. Your ability to successfully negotiate shorter terms will center on how badly the distributor wants to carry your record, and how much faith they have in your title's sell-through ability.

Regardless of the terms you secure, payment will transpire per the disbursement schedule set forth in your Distribution Agreement. Some standard elements apply to nearly all Distribution Agreements, such as the reserve or hold-back against returns. Some such hold-back clauses call for as high as 40% to 50% reserve to be maintained; some are as low as 10% or 20%. This serves as a protection for the distributor in the event that moderate to significant returns occur with your title. Let's say based on placement your distributor pays you after 90 days on 500 units; however, after their next billing cycle with retail they receive 200 returns on your title. They've over paid you, their only recourse now is to wait for the opportunity to take the difference out from future sales, or call you up and request that you cut a check back to them. Now let's say there was a 50% reserve held back; at the 90 day pay point you would receive payment for 250 units with payment for the balance held in a credit account for your label. At the end of that ensuing retail billing cycle when the returns came in, the distributor is not hurt and you are paid for the 50 units still outstanding after the deduction of 200 returns. Reading through this clause or line item in a contract, it seems complex when in fact, as you can see it's quite simple. Your Distribution Agreement will stipulate as to how long each hold back remains in reserve. Note that each payment disbursement will have a corresponding credit or deposit for credit in your account with the distributor. For example: if your Agreement calls for a 50% reserve to be held back for 120 days; that means that when the payable 50% is disbursed to you, the reserved 50% is credited to your account and the 120 day hold back time period begins.

PROTECT YOURSELF

Though not a common occurrence, sometimes, smaller independent distribution operations have been known to employ less than ethical tactics in dealing with small indie labels. The rule of thumb for dealing with a distributor is to only give them as many records as you can afford to lose. Some of these less than ethical practices include: not paying, losing your invoice, going out of business, etc. The best way to safeguard against such circumstances and protect yourself is keep your product selling. If sell-through is occurring the distributor will require additional units, request payment for the previous block of units prior to forwarding additional units to meet the demand. The best overall safeguard is to keep in constant contact with the distributor and be aware of how your release is doing at retail. Also, when your distributor places an order with you for additional units, always ask for a physical P.O. (*Purchase Order*) and corresponding P.O. number. Be diligent, prudent and use common sense, keep good comprehensive records of all transactions with your distributor.

INVOICING

If you have access to a computer, use it to make your invoices. For your internal reference and records, assign each outgoing invoice an invoice number. The idea is to make it look professional; companies tend to give greater respect and attention to professional looking documentation. No handwritten letters! Be sure to include their P.O. number and your invoice and clearly state the terms for payment agreed upon in the Distribution Agreement providing the due date for payment. You'll need to find out who handles the distributor's accounts payable and send your invoices to that person directly.

If you experience delays or problems receiving payment you know is due to you, tell them to send your records back. Then, inform them of your intent to submit the invoice to collection and call a few collection agencies in their area. If you've got the P.O. number and have properly invoiced the distributor, then you have a legitimate debt for collection. A collection agency will simply tack on their fee after obtaining payment from said distributor.

When you ship them your records, use the delivery confirmation service where UPS or the post office sends you proof that the distributor received your package.

REQUEST FOR RETURN
It is standard practice in the record industry for record companies to allow stores and distributors to return unsold records for credit against what they owe. If it's clear that a distributor is not going to pay you, demand that they return your goods. Most will probably want to return when it's time to pay you, anyway. Then, after they've sent them back, they'll turn around and order those same records back from you again! This is their way of avoiding spending cash on inventory that is sitting in their warehouse. When they re-order the records from you, they now have fresh 90-day (*or whatever*) terms to work with. One thing you must specify is that they pay freight on any returns.

GETTING STARTED
Before we get into the nitty-gritty of getting and maintaining good distribution, I want to give you a general overview of how it's all going to work. First, you're going to create what's called a "one- sheet"- a one-page description of your record that tells distributors and retailers why they should carry it. The first step is to create the "one-sheet" for your release. Recall from above that the purpose of the one-sheet is to convince distributors and retailers to stock your record, and to give them all the information they need to enter it into their computerized accounting and inventory systems. (*Beware: if your distributor is not using a computerized accounting and tracking system, they probably won't be able to keep track of where they've shipped your records or find out how many have sold.*)

Next, you're going to mail packages containing your record along with the one-sheet to the distributors in your area. Then this is the hard part, you're going to meet with them, either by phone or in person, and convince them to work with you.

Once you find a distributor who wants to work with your product and with whom you feel comfortable, you will enter into a business relationship with them by signing a Distribution Agreement, which is a short contract that outlines the terms and conditions of your business arrangement. At this point, the distributor will send you a purchase order, or "P.O.", for a quantity of units. You'll ship the units, and the distributor will try to convince stores within the area of your promotion or your designated launch territory to stock them.

The distributor will handle all the accounting, and will pay you for the records either when they need more records from you or when you decide to "recall" the release. If they need more records, they'll send you another P.O., and you'll ship them more records, that is if things go smoothly, in which you're shipping records (*by your band and maybe others as well*) to the distributor and in return the distributor is paying you for past shipments that have already sold at retail. The more records you have that the distributor wants, and the more copies of these records that are being ordered by retailers, the more attention you'll get from (*and the faster you'll be paid by*) the distributor.

DISTRIBUTORS AND ORGANIZATIONS

(NAIRD). Members of this organization are owners of independent labels, distributors and manufacturers. The AFIM organization publishes an annual directory of member distributors and labels. Plan to attend the AFIM's annual convention to meet and network with the distributors. Play your releases for them, acquaint them with your promotional and performance plans, and ask questions about their distribution services, procedures, policies and acceptance criterion. At the same time, you can speak with the owners of other labels that use independent distributors. It is in your interest to find out about different distributors' reputations for service and payment. Ask the owners of the stores that carry your products. They can often provide information as to what other labels their particular distributors carry and what their business reputation is in the marketplace. Ask artists that record in your genre of music, visit their web sites and the web sites of their affiliate labels. They often name their distributors or provide links to distributor web sites. Researching artists by name on the Internet can also lead to the names of distributors. Information about record distributors is available from associations devoted to particular genres of music and in many industry trade magazines that specialize in particular genres. You can find a list of recording distributors in The Billboard International Buyer's Guide Directory.

DISTRIBUTORS AND PROMOTION

Once you find a distributor you will have to work to keep that distributor interested in your recordings and working on your behalf, especially if you do not have a proven volume of sales. Think of the distributor as a business partner who is working with you to achieve a mutual goal: selling your recordings. News about your promotional successes and performances is important because distributors will use it as leverage to persuade stores to carry your product. This is called retail promotion, many distributors, especially those with very large catalogs, do not truly engage in this practice on your behalf. Even those that have sales teams are only pushing the catalog to retail not many individual titles within it are being pushed. This is what can set your release apart from the many others in the catalog. You must lend your diligent efforts in this regard. Send them all press releases, performance dates, radio data and promotional activity reports; offer to supply updated text for their one-sheets for your release, which are universally used by distributors as quick reference sheets. They contain the artist's name, name of the record, label's name, date of release and UPC bar code number and catalog number. They also provide a brief description of the recording, its genre, unique qualities, selling points, highlight well-known musicians, quotes from reviewers, and important tour dates.

52

In the last few years, several independent music product distributors have increased their services to supplement the promotional efforts of their labels. These include: sending out regular newsletters that feature tour dates, news of airplay, and clips from favorable reviews, paying for listening posts at retail record stores, booking concerts at retail outlets, taking out ads, sponsoring internet radio stations that feature music from the labels they carry, and linking their web site to internet music stores.

When you are going to tour in an area that is serviced by your distributor, tell them in advance so they can persuade stores to take extra stock and put up special displays. Offer to meet store owners and salespeople. Let the distributor know about your plans for getting reviews and airplay and ask them for suggestions. Even if you are not touring send your distributors all your press releases and favorable reviews to inform them of your progress. Find out about your distributors' salespeople and deal with them personally. Add them to your mailing list, phone them occasionally and visit them when you are in their area. If you deal with distributors that handle many different labels, you will find that the salespeople are not always acquainted with all the product they sell. Any input from you will give your title an extra push and it's generally serving the greater good to keep your release in their faces and on their minds.

DOING BUSINESS WITH A DISTRIBUTOR
The price at which distributors buy from record labels is commonly 50% to 55% of the retail list price. Variations are based on your discounting policies, leverage in the marketplace, and number of units sold. Written agreements with your distributors should specify the discounts, when and how often you will be paid, and the amount of promotional units you will provide for giveaways to sales personnel, retail, etc. Discounts as high as 60% are given to distributors for large volume buys. Distributors order inventory and,

being wary about paying for product that might be returned, specify that payment will not be made until the stores have paid them. Stores pay distributors on a monthly or quarterly basis; they return unsold merchandise, generally after 90 days. The label and distributor agree to take back unsold and defective units. This means the record label consigns units to distributors and the distributors consign them to the stores. Distributors make accountings to labels on a quarterly, semi-annual, or annual basis. They will want some free promotional records and want to make at least one copy available to each store they service as a way of introducing your product. Your written agreement with them should specify how many recordings they can make available as promotional giveaways or samples. Ensure that these copies are not just extras that will be returned for credit by using stickers that say "Promotional Copy, Not for Sale" or by otherwise distinguishing "promo" copies from sales copies. Once you have received an order from a distributor, you must ship or deliver the units at your expense. Include an invoice that states the terms of sale with each delivery.

COLLECTION

The biggest headache, in dealing with distributors is the long wait for payment. Their primary reason will be that store payments are delayed. To expedite payment distributors may offer incentives such as an additional 10% to 15% discount for cash on delivery with returns accepted only for damaged merchandise or a sliding scale discount and a one-for-ten policy. The label gives the distributor a free unit for every 10 bought and paid for within a specified period, usually 30 days. Distributors assess stores for late payment, usually 2% to 5% of the amount owing. You can use some of these same tactics with a distributor.

Many labels report that a period of six months is common before they see the first payment for new inventory and there are distributors (*and stores*) that delay payments for a year or more or never pay; a practice that has occurred often enough to warrant warning you about it here. The practice is often discriminatory: the distributors first pays labels whose products sell faster than others and those that have done business with them for a longer period of time. They will often delay payments to new labels or labels with sloppy business practices or less professional administrative conduct. Collecting money is one of the least appealing aspects of selling. If you are not persistent distributors will think that you do not care when you are paid. The labels that are the most persistent are usually paid in a more timely manner. It is very important to find out something about distributors' payment reputations before you deal with them. Ask Owners of other recording labels. People are usually willing to share their experiences, particularly the negative ones. You have real leverage to collect only when your recordings are selling quickly and your distributor must reorder or when you put out a second recording to follow a record that has sold well. Many labels report cutting off distributors from receiving more product the very first time payments lapse beyond 90 days. This may sound hard-nosed, but it is accepted as prudent business practice and lets companies know you are not willing to be taken advantage of. You can expedite the collection process only through constant diligence. Develop a personal working relationship with key personnel. Visit and talk to your distributors as often as you can. Tell them about your performance and promotional successes as they occur or in advance. Regular and personable communication is the best method for assuring they will not neglect you. Always put an audit clause in your agreements that specifies you have the right to visit their accounting offices once during a calendar year and audit their books for your account.

Sell or consign only small numbers of units to distributors at first, so if sales increase rapidly and the distributor will need more recordings to keep up with demand, you can refuse to provide them until the last consignment is paid for. Your chances of getting paid are better anyway, since the amounts involved are small. Distributors know their retail accounts and can often make fairly accurate estimates about the rate of sale for your release. Their initial order will be based on that knowledge and further based on your promotional outlook and marketing plan.

Be extremely diligent about collections. If distributors miss an accounting period, send the distributor a certified letter stating that they missed the payment date. Start phoning and ask to talk to the accountant. If you are told repeatedly that the accountant is "out of the office," complain to the person on the phone. Keep bothering them.   Recognize that you are financing the distributor.   Not getting paid on time means that they are using your money for maintaining their own cash flow or other inventory management issues not related to your product.

An alternative to trying to expedite the collection process is, to simply accept the fact that you have to wait to be paid. Even so, you must put limits on what you will accept.   The foregoing is not meant to discourage you from using a distributor, but to inform you that it often takes awhile for money to get back to you, so plan accordingly. Always have some reserve; never expend everything in hopes that you will be paid before you will need additional units pressed. When you do find distributors that sell your product for you and pay on time, acknowledge them graciously. Consider any move to a new distributor very carefully, weigh possible profits against the loyalty and hard work of your current distributor.

CHAPTER 6

Distribution Resources

RETAIL CATALOGS AND DATABASES

Once you offer your recording for sale, you qualify for listing in recording catalogs and databases that list information about recordings. Retailers, to locate and order product for their outlets frequently review such resources. It is important to be listed so retail can become aware of your product and order it directly through your distributor.

MUZE

It is a must to send over your new release information to Muze, just as it is to send your new release info to Soundscan and your album to BDS, getting your release into each system.

Muze is an organization that brings information solutions to entertainment retailers. It is very important for you, the label to forward any new releases to Muze. The best way is to give them a (*one-sheet*), the retail ready album and a cover letter stating the release date, title of album, artist, name of label, name of the distributor, and to formally ask Muze to put your release into their database. The Muze editors and programmers continuously enhance industry data about all commercially available music, books and videos with critical annotations, authoritative assessments, expert classification and smart data design.

The History of Muze; co-founded by Paul Zullo and Trev Huxley, Muze began with seed money supplied in part by the Grateful Dead's Bob Weir. Current majority owners, John W. Kluge and Stuart Subotnick, partners in the privately held Metromedia Company now closely hold Muze.

Since 1991, when first in-store music information system began a revolution in American music retailing, sellers and consumers alike have enjoyed the benefits of Muze's unique combination of information, editorial intelligence and user-friendly technology. Building on their success as a valued provider of music information, Muze added movies and then books to their core database.   In 1995 they pioneered computer-driven server technology for in-store listening with Muze SD. As the World Wide Web began to have a major impact on business success in the retail environment, Muze launched its first e-commerce venture in 1996, when West Coast Entertainment chose Muze video data to power their Internet-linked in-store information centers. Over the past three years, Muze data has been adopted by more than 90% of on-line music destinations, including Amazon, Yahoo! and Snap.

You will need to forward your new release information to:

Muze Inc.
304 Hudson Street
8th Floor
New York
New York 10013
Tel (212) 824-0300
Fax (212) 741-1246

The Phonolog published by Muze, Inc. is a comprehensive loose-leaf catalog that lists currently available recordings cross-referenced by label, title, artist, and category. Subscribers receive weekly updates. Phonolog print listings are also accessible by using Muze's software, Phonolog for Windows.

Muze also publishes Muze for Music.   It is a comprehensive music database that is available as an in-store interactive information system for traditional retailers, and as a licensable database for on-line retailers. This database contains over 200,000 music titles and associated album information, including title, artist, label, catalog number, length of recording, track list, liner notes, reviews, etc. Both album and song titles are searchable by key words.

Listings in Phonolog, and Muze for Music, are free and open to all recordings for sale and generally available in record stores. To be listed, send a copy of your recording, including associated packaging, along with production notes and promotional materials. The Schwann Artist, an annual guide to Classical performers, and Schwann Opus, a quarterly Classical guide organized by composer and piece, list CDs and cassettes currently available in the United States. The Schwann Spectrum, a quarterly guide to non-classical listings, was recently redesigned and resumed publication in 1999 following a period of unavailability.

Listings in Schwann publications are free, but recordings must be available through a U.S. telephone number and address or be distributed nationally to stores. In order to be listed, labels must send a copy of their recording(s) and information about the record company (*name, address, phone number, contact person*).

The addresses for these catalogs are listed in the Directory of Resources. When you forward your materials and information to the catalogs, include the names and addresses of distributors that list your recording. List all information as it is shown on your product label, "A" side first.

SOUNDSCAN
What is Soundscan? Soundscan is an online information system that tracks actual music sales throughout the Unites States. Soundscan information first became available on January 1, 1991. Currently all of the major music labels and most of the independent labels subscribe to Soundscan. The Billboard Magazine charts are constructed directly from Soundscan data in part.

Sales information is gathered from over 14,000 reporters (*retail and mass merchandisers*), which is compiled and made available on a weekly basis. Soundscan clients include record labels, distribution companies, artist managers, booking agents, concert promoters and venue owners.

There are two packages available to Soundscan subscribers. The first is a full access package and the second is a limited access package. Full access is unlimited access to Soundscan data, 24 hour access to the database, and an unlimited number of log-ons. Limited access subscribers have access only to the information on their label's product, and are limited to (20) titles. The client requirements are that the subscribers must pay for both system access and chart access fees. Soundscan information cannot be sold to non-subscribers.

How it Works
Data is sent from the point-of-sale cash registers via modem from the stores to Soundscan each week. The information is then available for PC downloading each Wednesday morning. Data files consist of store type, piece counts and the Universal Product Code (UPC)

NORTH LEXINGTON AVENUE, 14TH FL.
WHITE PLAINS, NY 10601
(914) 684-5500
FAX (914) 684-5606

[X]

TITLE ADDITION SHEET

To add a title to the SOUNDSCAN database, each field on the title addition sheet must be completed in order for it to be accepted. Please use a separate form for each additional title.

Title: _____
Release Date: _____

Artist: _____

Label Information as it applies to this product

Parent Label: _____
Distribution Co. _____

Sub Label: _____
Label Abbr: __ __ __ __

Please enter all **digits of the** U.P.C. Code. **(Including** Prefix and Suffix**)**
To enter identification codes on how your product should be listed please check the example below.

PLEASE PRINT IN ONE CONFIGURATION FOR EACH LINE.

U.P.C. Code

EXAMPLE Configurations Types		PRICE	TYPE
9 9 9 9 9 9 9 9 9 9	9	9.99	A
_ _ _ _ _ _ _ _ _ _	_	____	___
_ _ _ _ _ _ _ _ _ _	_	____	___
_ _ _ _ _ _ _ _ _ _	_	____	___

ALBUM   **SINGLES**
A= LP 12" LP   E=CD SINGLE
B=CASS. LP   F=LP 12"
C=CD LP   G=CASS. SINGLE
D=DVD AUD   I=CD MAXI
VIDEO
M=VHS
L=DVD

PLEASE SELECT THE GENRE WHICH APPLIES TO THIS PRODUCT:

_____ 150 - R & B   _____ 520 - SOUNDTRACK
_____ 400 - COUNTRY   _____ 184 - WORLD
_____ 500 - JAZZ   _____ 100 - ROCK
_____ 186 - LATIN   _____ 620 - COMEDY
_____ 102 - METAL   _____ 640 - GOSPEL
_____ 200 - CLASSICAL   _____ 630 - CHRISTIAN
_____ 152 - RAP   _____ 625 - KARAOKE
_____ 180 - REGGAE   _____ 360 - NEW AGE
_____ 690 - CHILDREN   _____ 156 -
DANCE/ELECTRONIC
_____ 470 - BLUES   _____ 178 - SKA

Your Name: _____ PH# (_____)_____-
_____ FAX# (_____)_____-_____
Email: _____

Please enter your name, phone number and fax number in case we have any questions.

62

BDS

BDS is Broadcast Data Systems, and is owned by Billboard. Using a patented computer technology, BDS monitors radio and television broadcasts, identifying songs and commercials as they are being aired. Unlike other monitoring systems, BDS technology requires no special encoding of the broadcast material or manipulation of signals. The computers actually "listen" to the stations electronically.

Each BDS monitor stores thousands of unique electronic "fingerprints". A fingerprint is a pattern created by BDS computers for each song in the system. As a station plays a song, the digitized broadcast signal is compared with the pattern library. Once the remote computer has recognized a song pattern, the system identifies the exact time, date and station for that play. Overnight the pattern library is updated and the day's detection history is transmitted from the remote sites to the central operations facility. By early morning, BDS processes the detection data collected from all of its field monitors and electronically redistributes the information to its clients' computers where it appears in report format for analysis.

The BDS Music Group services the music industry through its Record Track and Radio Track product lines. What exactly is a song pattern? Patterns can be of different lengths, depending on the situation. They can be made from any part of the song. The computer "listens" to the song in its entirety and selects a cross-section that has the greatest amount of unique audio information from which to make identification. That section is used to create the digital "fingerprint" or pattern. Sound to the human ear has no relation to sound as the BDS computer hears it. However, if one song samples another one and uses a large enough piece of it, it is possible that BDS could detect the originally patterned track rather that the new one. In that case, a pattern can be made that avoids the sample section.

63

The BDS systems can usually handle increases in speed up to 4%. Occasionally a station speeds up a record so much that the BDS computer no longer recognizes it. In that situation, BDS will make an additional pattern at a higher speed so as to properly identify the track.

If a mix version is sent from the label to be encoded in the system, or if a station does its own edit or mix and does not provide BDS with a copy, it is possible that a BDS computer will not recognize that mix when it is played on the air. However, it is also possible that it will recognize it. There is no definitive way to know.
As a label or station all music for encoding to BDS should be sent to:

BDS
8100 NW 101st Terrace
Kansas City, MO 64153
(Attention: Encoding)
(DAT, CD, CD single, 12" Vinyl, LP, Reel, cassette, tapes, video and radio re-mixes)

UPC / BAR CODE

HOW TO GET A UPC NUMBER FOR YOUR PRODUCT?
The short answer is, in the USA call (937) 435-3870, the Uniform Code Council. For a fee, the Uniform Code Council will issue you a company number and send you a packet of information about how to use it. You can also go online at: www.uccouncil.org

Uniform Code Council, Inc
7887 Washington Village Drive, Suite 300
Dayton, OH 45459
937-435-3870
937-435-7317

HOW TO GET A BAR CODE FOR YOUR PRODUCT
When someone asks this question, they are talking

about the UPC or EAN symbol found on most retail products around the world. Specifically, they are asking how to obtain a Universal Product Code Identification Number, which they can encode into a UPC-A or EAN-13 bar code symbol on their product. EAN stands for European Article Number, which has 13-digits. In the US your record label should first obtain a unique six-digit company identification number by becoming a member of the Uniform Code Council.

A full set of technical specifications and guidelines will be provided with your number. They also will provide a list of suppliers that can produce camera-ready bar code symbols than can be included in the product's package graphics. You can assign the 5-digit product code yourself. The number assigned to each product your company produces must be unique. For example, if you have two different sizes of the same product, each must be assigned a different number. When you assign the numbers, you should communicate them to your affiliates, distributors and other partners.

You do not have to be incorporated to apply for a UPC company number. In other words, you can apply for a number as a sole proprietor. However, the Uniform Code Council recommends that you register your business name before applying. The way you register your name varies from state to state. Often when you apply for a business license, you will also be required to "register" the name of the business. In any event, the UCC does not require this to become a member.

The Uniform Code Council (UCC) issues numerical company and product configuration codes to standardize computerized tracking of sales and inventory. On a CD for example you will see a bar code which has 12 numbers and vertical bars, which at checkout from a retail store, the bar code is scanned (via Soundscan technology) and placed into the computer database as a reflection of that sale. It will also be compiled into sales statistics industry wide. Lets break down the 12-digit numbers: The first (6) belong to the record label, the next (4) is the Catalog

Number, which you as the label will create a unique number for each album, a way to facilitate tracking throughout the ordering, distribution, and billing processes. The next number if the product is a CD is always the number 2, and for cassette the number 4, if it is vinyl it will be 1. Lastly, is the Check digit number, the very last number. This digit lets the scanner determine if it scanned the number correctly or not. Here is a mathematical formula to use to create the check digit number:

1. Add together the value of all the digits in odd positions (digits1, 3, 5, 7, 9, and 11). So 6 + 9 + 8 + 0 + 9 = 32.
2. Multiply that number by 3. So 32 x 3 = 96.
3. Add together the value of all the digits in even positions (digits 2, 4, 6, 8, 10). So 3 + 3 + 2 + 0 + 3 = 11.
4. Add this sum to the value in Step 2. So 96 + 11 = 107.
5. Take the number in Step 4. To create the check digit, determine the number that, when added to the number in Step 4, is multiple of 10. So 107 + 3 = 110, and the check digit is therefore 3.

Each time the scanner scans an item, the scanner performs this calculation. If the check digit it calculates is different from the check digit it reads, the scanner knows that something went wrong and the item needs to be re-scanned.

Now the good news, there is a much faster way of coming up with the check digit number. Go online to Google or any other search engine and type in the word (Barcodem), here you will be able to see, for example a program called Sam's Bar code Maker, download it, and you are ready to make your own bar code. This program is a FREE trial for 30-days or you can purchase it for usually around $35 dollars. With this program you just put in the 11-digit numbers and it creates the bar code in seconds, in which you can save as a tiff, bitmap or JPEG file to forward over to your graphics department for use in the artwork for your CD.

INDEPENDENT DISTRIBUTION

NATIONAL ASSOCIATION OF INDEPENDENT RECORD DISTRIBUTORS (NAIRD)

A half dozen or so major multinationals handle the preponderant share of record distribution in the United States. But they don't do it all. A share of the business is in the hands of independent distributors, who provide services for hundreds of independent labels. Independent distributors usually provide promotion services as well. Some independents are just order-takers. Others have a staff of enterprising salespeople and merchandisers who call on record stores, deliver merchandise, and set up displays, for instance, much like the major label branch offices do.

There are regional independent distributors as well as national independent distributors, some of whom have evolved through a merger or confederation of regional distributors. Large independent distributors are confronted with pleas from new firms to take on yet another line. -If they consider adding new labels, management must determine whether it has the capacity to handle the increased inventory and the will to tie up additional working capital on unproven suppliers. If they stocked every recording that appears promising, they would soon go broke. But if they fail to stock new product that suddenly bursts wide open at the retail level, their local accounts will sometimes bypass the local distributor and buy directly from the record manufacturer. These kinds of management decisions have been poorly handled by many distributors. They are now out of business. Since 1972, the interests of these independent companies have been represented by NAIRD, the National Association of Independent Record Distributors'. The association was originally organized to set up a distribution network and to "form a unified voice in the industry for small labels and independent distributors. Its national conventions provide small firms a convenient place for the exchange of information and for the forming of distribution arrangements for companies not affiliated with the major labels and their distribution networks.

One-Stops. One-stops are a special kind of distributor. They came into being in the 1940s mainly to accommodate the needs of juke- box operators. A one-stop is a distributor who handles all labels, including the majors. One-stops are set up to service not only jukebox operators, but small rack jobbers and mom-and-pop retailers. Most of these customers place small orders, often dropping by to pick up the merchandise themselves. Because of the low volume of sales per customer, and because one-stops must purchase records from distributors, one-stops cannot offer as good a discount as a full-line distributor. But their customers pay the higher prices because they appreciate the convenience of a one-stop operation. One-stops sell more labels, in fewer quantities but at a higher price than the traditional independent distributors.

NATIONAL ASSOCIATION OF RECORDING MERCHANDISERS (NARM)

The National Association of Recording Merchandisers (NARM)- headquartered in Marlton, NJ is the international trade association that represents the recorded music distribution industry. More than 1,000 companies are NARM members. Individuals automatically become members when their companies join. The two categories of company membership are:

1. Regular members: This category includes retailers, rack jobbers, one stops, independent distributors, and other wholesalers.

2. Associate members: This category includes manufacturers and suppliers of music, video, and other forms of recorded entertainment, as well as suppliers of other accessories, products, and services utilized by recording merchandisers such as display fixtures, advertising, printing, packaging, security systems, and computer hardware and software. All companies who join NARM pay annual dues based on their yearly sales volume. Member benefits include: Annual Convention-a forum for recording merchandisers and manufacturers to network and discuss mutual opportunities and concerns. Merchandising Campaigns-NARM supplies point-of-purchase materials free to its members, as well as educational videos on merchandising. NARM schedules additional

conferences and meetings for its members and it aggressively lobbies to represent members' interest in local, state, and federal legislative matters.

CHAPTER 7

Alternative Selling and Total Exposure

CUTOUTS, REPACKAGING

Recording companies / labels often find it difficult to estimate how many records to press for the initial release or re-supply of a particular product. If they underestimate demand, consumers cannot be accommodated. If they overestimate demand, they will find their warehouses stocked with dormant, inactive merchandise. Once the demand drops sharply on a given title, the decision is made to stop production. The inventory remaining is known as cutout product. Retail outlets cannot move this stock at normal prices because clearly, consumer interest has waned. At this point, distributors find it prudent to unload this merchandise at cost or below cost on buyers who specialize in cutouts. These cutout merchants buy bulk quantities, warehouse the units, then vend them to rack jobbers and other retailers at a very low price; "cutout price". Their clients, in turn, offer these cutouts at extremely low prices. Both parties usually turn a profit through volume, and the retail consumer gets a bargain, but artists do not generally receive royalties on cutouts.

Some record stores find that their revenues from cutouts are better than from conventional sales and they are of course priced to sell volume. Some cutout companies buy or lease old masters, then re-release titles or fallen artists who still have loyal fans ready to consume dated favorites at bargain prices. For example, for years cutout merchants and re-packagers were able to sell "re-releases" or "new" releases of the big band hits of the 1940s. Another perennial repertoire comes from the early rock and roll hits. Reissues of country music also continue to sell, through "new" releases, new packages, or cutouts.

Perhaps the most successful merchandising of old and

repackaged hits is seen on television. Companies buy up or lease masters from recording companies holding the rights to old hits, then repackage them under their own labels. These companies often own immense libraries of dated recordings. These re-packagers favor such titles as "Hits of the 1980s", "Sinatra's Greatest Hits" or "The Best of Country Music." They produce low-cost, hard-sell TV spots, obtain time on TV and cable, and provide a mailing address and toll-free telephone number for viewers to place their orders through massive mail-order or direct sales (DS) / direct response (DR) campaigns. Some operators in this field manage to promote repackaging deals without clearly defined licensing arrangements. The 1976 Copyright Act made it easier to control and regulate operations of this kind.

MAIL ORDER
Sales can be generated through mailings to people on your fan list and rented mailing lists, and through mail-order catalogs that specialize in your musical genre, recordings in general, or sell a variety of merchandise. Success depends on accurately assessing your audience, researching and obtaining the appropriate mailing lists, and sending out advertising packages that effectively communicate your message. Mail-order information should also be included in the printed materials for your recording if you choose to make it available in this manner to the buying public.

If your goal is to sell just to fans that are already interested in your music, your fan base, an attractively designed mail-order form may be all that you need. Add shipping and handling fees to the price of the recording; and provide your customers with shipping choices. That fee should cover the cost of shipping, the mailer, and the time spent preparing the package and administratively logging the sale for tax and business purposes.

If you want to interest others, have your graphic

71

designer prepare a special mailing package that uses the graphic elements from your product cover and promotional materials. This package should include a business reply card or return postage paid envelope. The easier and less time consuming you make it for people to respond to you, the higher your sales will be. Independent label owners have found that the number of responses to mail order offerings are higher when more than one title is offered or when the offer includes complementary items like T-shirts, decals and posters. If you are attempting to capitalize on the Christmas buying season, advertisements should be mailed no later than October 15. You can save money and increase sales by doing a cooperative mailing with other independent labels.

Advertising your release in trade and consumer music publications is a way to get radio airplay, sell records and announce tours. Advertising can get very expensive, very quickly, and for the independent label this could mean a lot of wasted money. Obviously, it all depends on how much money you have to spend. Conduct your own analysis of ad costs vs. sales potential before taking out any ad, ask yourself how many records can this ad realistically sell? Determine your "break even point; how many units you must sell as a result of the ad to cover the cost of the ad. If you don't think it will make more money than it will cost, you probably shouldn't take out the ad. Base this decision on exposure, how many viewers, listeners or readers will the ad effectively reach; how many potential consumers will get your intended message? If you don't have nationwide distribution, don't take out a $1000 ad in a national publication unless you honestly think you can make that expenditure back through mail order alone. No matter how great your release is, if people haven't heard of you they most likely will not be shelling out 15 bucks or so for your CD. That $1000 could pay for dozens of co-op ads with local record stores, or smaller ads in regional music magazines; more suitable, targeted marketing. You've got to think about where your advertising dollar will do the most good. Wherever you place your ads, to release any record successfully you are going to have to spend dollars on some sort of advertising.

AD PLACEMENT

Where should those ads be placed? First, get ad rate information from magazines in which you're interested in advertising (*this is also a great way to get free subscriptions to your favorite magazines*). The cost of the ad space will probably be the deciding factor as well as your analysis of their subscriber base. If you have a local music magazine or entertainment weekly in your area, that would be a good place to start.

You may be surprised to find that the smallest, cheapest ad you placed got the biggest response. Targeting the ads specifically to the audience you're trying to reach is the key here. Even a cheap, catchy classified ad offering a free catalog may get a response from hundreds of interested music fans. If it's possible, taking out an ad in an issue in which a review of your record will appear is always timely and effective. It's kind of the one-two punch effect. If you're going to be sending your release out to national radio, a radio send-out can be maximized by a few, well-placed ads in college trade publications such as CMJ. These ads get music directors and DJs interested in your record.

INDIE AD DISCOUNTS

Many publications offer discounts to independent labels and bands. ASK FOR IT! Also, if you can, get terms with the magazine rather than pay cash in advance. If you can defer paying for the ad for a few months, you may be able to make enough money selling your releases through mail order to cover the cost of the ad within your agreed upon billing cycle.

CHAPTER 8

THE INTERNET

CREATING YOUR MUSIC WEBSITE

Having your own music website active and visible increases your chances of more exposure and possible sale of your music, not to mention you may also be creating a fan following. Investing in a website designer would be money well spent. If this is not within your budget, post a sign at a local college for an intern to design your site. It is very important to have it done professionally, not to mention the search engines do not recognize "Do it yourself" website services where they let you build your site through Java scripts. The search engine "spiders" pass by the given "Meta-tags" in the site, and recognize it as a free Website Host Provider, therein limiting your chances of higher search engine placement. This is critical, since it is all about being in the first or second page of a search result.

SEARCH ENGINES

There are several free services that will place your URL, or web address, in multiple search engines for free. New and improving services can change almost every day, it is highly recommended that you go to **www.google.com**. Once you are there just type in "free search engines submittal". In addition, adding your URL manually to **www.google.com**, **www.yahoo.com**, **www.msn.com**, and **www.hotbot.com**, just to name a few will also increase your URL's viewership. Also recommended is adding your band to **www.iuma.com**, which receives well over 100,000 hits each day.

ONLINE MUSIC DISTRIBUTION

The two best services found online to sell your CD would be **www.cdbaby.com** and **www.amazon.com**. You will have to self-administrate your titles, it is very easy and fast. Both services actually report to Soundscan, which is a plus.

CDBaby.com even takes it a step further by giving to you the customer's email address and physical address when a purchase of your title occurs, another way of adding to your loyal fan database and conducting analysis of your advertising, along with the consumer demographic you are reaching.

EMAIL CAMPAIGNS

They say that the internet is the great leveler and it is true. There is no better evidence of that than email. What sets the majors apart from the indies is there ability to reach millions of people, potential consumers with vast expenditures on broad sweeping advertising and promotional campaigns. Thanks to the internet, and specifically email, essentially for the $19.99 to $39.99 fee for internet service, any label or artist can potentially reach the same number of consumers. You can put together an email mailing list the same way you would a normal mailing list. You can harvest email addresses from other labels, web sites, bands you know, or simply purchase them for literally pennies per thousand addresses. When purchasing addresses you can even tailor your list to include only persons possibly predisposed to music buying or R&B listeners or, whatever. With the click of a button you can send press releases, tour schedules or show announcements, even track samples to hundreds or thousands, or hundreds of thousands of people at once, and at virtually no cost. The savings over traditional mass flier mailings is exponential and you could not possibly mail that many fliers through conventional mail with any sort of cost efficiency.

NEWSGROUPS

Newsgroups are online discussion groups or message boards stored on servers all over the world. You can "subscribe" to these newsgroups through your internet service provider using a news reader program (*like Netscape News*). There are literally tens of thousands of newsgroups online; a great many devoted to music. Additionally, most colleges have discussion groups and message boards through online newsgroups. The subjects covered by individual newsgroups are endless, from guitars to Peacocks. There are newsgroups devoted to hundreds of different famous (*and non-famous*) bands. People "post" messages or questions on these newsgroups, and then other people read them and respond and then other people respond to those responses, and so on. You can also create new groups.

Check out, alt.music.independent, for questions and advice about putting out your own music. Got a question about an indie label? Need information on cheap CD manufacturing? Need a place to play in Topeka? You can get these answers and lots more by subscribing to music-related newsgroups.

Use the internet as a reference tool. Almost every major label and large independent label has a website, as do most music related organizations. ASCAP (http://www.ascap.com) and BMI (http://www.bmi.com) both have sites that can give you information on performance rights and music publishing. CMJ (College Music Journal) also has a website you can use to view their college radio charts at http://www.cmjmusic.com.

If you're new to the Net, a good place to start is the IMusic section at Yahoo! (http://www. yahoo.com). It's a pretty comprehensive directory of music-related websites, broken down into dozens of categories. There are also several sites devoted solely to musicians who are releasing their own music. One is Outersound, ASCAP's site, lets you search their song title database. (http://www.outersound.com), which is set up like a city for independent musicians, featuring areas on recording, touring, manufacturing records, and lots more. A good site for touring bands is WilMA, the Worldwide Internet Live Music Archive (http://www.wilma.com). Its "Search-O-Matic" feature is an interactive database of artists, venues and concert listings from thousands of clubs. Again, check Yahoo under the "Independent Music" category for more useful music sites.

INTERNET RADIO
Many college and commercial radio stations also

broadcast over the Internet. Using free software like RealAudio (http://www.realaudio.com) you can listen to stations all over the world with FM-quality sound. Internet radio is quickly becoming a great new outlet for independent music to get heard with some internet radio stations legitimately boasting hundreds of thousands of listeners. You can find a list of Internet radio sites on Yahoo and get information about submitting your music to them.

CONCLUSION

The key to getting your message across in an email campaign is to get people to actually look at the ad, so make it as blatant and eye-catching as possible. Always include contact information and a free catalog offer when doing any type of campaign. Even if you only have one release, you can make some sort of propaganda sheet to send to people who respond. You should also include information on how a reader can order your record through the mail, and if your band is touring, include the performance dates and venue information. If you've got a web site that features an online catalog, always include the address in your ads. This is an easy way for people all over the world to get more information about you and your release. The newest, and possibly the best new advertising medium for independent musicians is the Internet.

There's been plenty of talk about how the Internet is revolutionizing the music industry, and guess what, it is true. The Internet, the international computer network, has become a great way for musicians to network and promote their music. There are dozens of online discussion groups that deal with issues facing independent labels and musicians, and all the big commercial online services (American Online, Compuserve, etc.) have music forums. If you have access to a computer, get Internet access, make it work for you!

CHAPTER 9

Radio

BREAK IT DOWN

Excluding internet radio for the moment, there are really only two types of radio stations you need be concerned with: commercial, and non-commercial (*public, NPR* [non-profit radio] *and College*). Of the two, you have a more realistic chance initially of getting your music played on college and public radio. People at these stations are generally more receptive to independently released, unknown artists. These stations are looking for new music; they want to be the ones who "discover" a major new artist. College radio should be your initial target. There are several hundred college stations that are substantial enough in their market to make a difference. Many of these stations are CMJ core stations, reporting their airplay data to CMJ for charting purposes.

Commercial radio is your secondary target; commercial radio airplay sells records. Commercial radio tends to be more conservative when it comes to taking chances on new bands; generally they don't. The giant broadcast corporations that own them typically govern their playlists, and without a track record or any degree of success at the non-commercial level, you will not make their playlists. They usually wait until a release proves itself in the college radio arena before they will consider adding it to their playlist. With this in mind, it makes more sense to put your efforts into college and public radio first, and then worry about commercial radio.

THE IMPORTANCE OF RADIO AIRPLAY

Almost every college in the U.S. has a student-run radio station. They range from one watt, carrier current stations, which can only be heard on campus, to 100,000 watt stations with a range or broadcast radius of over 100 miles. The one thing they have in common is that they will broadcast music from unknown, unproven bands and artists. Also, most

78

college stations have dozens of different specialty shows that feature almost every style of music to match the diversity of the student body. The listeners of these shows are devoted music fans, and are probably your biggest potential audience. In recent years, the major corporate labels have pumped millions of dollars of advertising and promotion into the college market in an attempt to influence what gets played. Take one look at today's college radio top ten and you'll realize that they've succeeded, to a degree. There are still hundreds of independent labels getting airplay all over the country, and some compete directly with the major label releases in this regard. Fortunately, college radio still remains more about the music thus keeping the playing field level.

For the independent artist, getting college (*or any*) radio airplay is extremely important. Getting your music heard across the country will open substantial opportunities related to exposure and sales. If your goal is to garner a major label deal, these labels pay close attention to the college charts, and use them as a prospecting sheet for new bands. CMJ is the number one source for the introduction of new music releases and independent artists on the rise. Although achieving chart debut on one of CMJ's many charts requires cumulative spins / airplay on perhaps 50 to 150 individual stations, it is not difficult to attain, especially with a good radio campaign. Playlists from the stations that are playing your record are also an impressive addition to your press kit. They are necessary to convince distributors to carry your music, as well as persuade commercial stations to give you a shot. If you want to do a nationwide tour or sell your records to stores in other parts of the country, you need to be getting some sort of radio airplay, period.

TRADES

There are several publications, which keep track of music getting played on the radio. Among them are College Music Journal (CMJ), Hits Magazine, Records & Radio (R&R), and Billboard. Stations report their top 20 or 30 songs (*based on spin count*) to these magazines, which compile the data into national radio charts. They also accept advertising, and a call or letter to any of the above will get you a sample copy and ad rates (*see Press list*).

These trade publications are read by Music Directors, (*they decide what music gets played*) Program Directors, (*they decide when and how often it gets played*) DJs (*they play their own personal choices along with a playlist determined by the MD and PD*) and other record labels. Advertisements placed in these publications are different than ads in consumer magazines, and should be targeted directly at the radio station personnel. (*E.g. "The new single from band X, on your desk now! Play it!"*) These ads should be timed to appear when your record arrives at the station and for several weeks after. This will help to distinguish your release from the dozens of others that stations receive each week. If it's a great ad, it can generate airplay and interest from stations, distributors, etc. These publications also print directories of bands and labels, so ask them for information on how to be included for listing.

RADIO MAIL OUT
Directories of non-commercial and commercial stations are available from several of the radio trade magazines. Do your homework, get sample copies of as many trades as you can, examine each station's playlist to see if your style of music will fit in with their format. This may seem time consuming but it will save you dollars on postage; if you send your materials to a station that does not play your genre, you have done so wastefully. You'll also be able to find out which stations are currently reporting to the trades and to which ones. Concentrate your promotional efforts on the reporting stations. Airplay in general is good; however, airplay on reporting stations will get you charted and possibly a review in a trade.

Send your release to all the stations that play your style of music. If this proves to be financially problematic, begin by sending it to those stations in your market or region.

WHAT TO SEND

In recent years, CDs have basically taken over as the format for radio, although many college stations as well as commercial mix-show DJs still actively play vinyl. Cassettes, whether they are cassette singles or full- length releases, are going to get substantially less airplay than CDs and vinyl, if at all. In order to add further assurance that once your package arrives it is actually considered, always first identify the MD or PD at the station and address your package to this person's attention. Re-sends are quite common, especially at larger stations, so be prepared to send additional packages in follow-up. Call each station, let the MD or PD know that you have just mailed them a new music package and it should arrive at the station shortly. Follow up with a call the following week just to confirm that they have received it; this is also a good time to pitch your release to them. Even if it seems as though they're immediately disinterested, they are more likely to actually listen to your track after having these couple of (*very brief*) conversations with you.

It is always better to send CD singles to radio stations. It should be a standard 5" CD with one or two tracks on them. The track information should be printed professionally on the CD face, do not include any artwork or CD jacket material as with a retail CD. Be sure to send it in a standard jewel case with a spine. The idea is to make as acceptable to the station as possible. If you have ever been in a station you know that CDs are stored in racks, an entire wall of CDs, the slots take standard jewel cases only and the only visible part is the spine. These CD singles are good for radio, and should be viewed as a vital promotional expense. Most CD manufacturers have special low replication rates for these radio singles.

When dealing with college radio it is important to remember that every station has many different specialty shows or segments; the rap show, hardcore show, reggae, etc. Make sure to write what style of music your track is on the outside of your package. Also, try to send it directly to the individual at the station in charge of that specific type of programming.

If you are not sending a single to radio, pick the song you feel is the strongest (*strongest for radio play*) on the album. Hi-light this track, both on the CD and in your conversations, emails or messages to the MD or PD. They will listen to the song that you have suggested as the main single to play. You should also ask to be added to the station's mailing list to receive their playlists. Also include postcards or posters, which will more than likely be placed inside the radio station, and not tossed out, again exposing and advertising your label and the release.

Another idea is to include a stamped, self-addressed postcard, which reads "If you'd like to receive more new releases from X Records fill out and return this postcard". On the card, ask for the station name, address and phone number, the name of the person who opened your package, their position at the station, etc. Now you'll have the name and number of someone you can call to see how your record is doing. This is a good way of finding out exactly who gives a damn about your release, then follow it up with a phone call about clubs and stores in the area, if they liked the record, etc. One thing you should always take into consideration when sending to college radio is that these are schools; many stations are closed down or run by a skeleton crew over the summer and winter vacations. Don't send your records during these months! The best times to send are usually September to November or February to May.

RADIO TOURING SUPPORT
Most college stations sponsor shows on campus or in their city. If a station is already playing your record, there's a good chance they would be willing to assist you further by possibly helping you put a show together in their town or even on campus. Always ask about doing an on-air interview or sending in a pre-recorded "liner" (*Hey ANY University, your listening to X Band on WANY*). Interviews are free airtime and are great advertisements for your show as well as sales support. Many stations will give away copies of your

release, so ask about it, offer to send in promotional materials or even retail CDs for on air giveaways. For the cost of a few CDs, you'll be getting airplay, advertising your band or show and gaining a few more fans in that area.

Touring is without a doubt the best way to promote your band. Besides being able to meet and play in front of people you've never seen before, touring gives you a captive audience to which you can sell your records, T-shirts and other band merchandise.

CHAPTER 10

Promotional Campaigns, Planning

TOURING AND BOOKING AGENTS

EVERY band or artist should be performing, especially if you've got product in stores. Not doing so is equivalent to not supporting your own release. It can be difficult for indies with unknown artists to obtain bookings. A good manager can help in this regard but you will inevitably want to find a booking agent. There are booking agents who specialize in arranging tours for new bands, but unless these people are approaching you, it's usually very hard to get them interested in a band no one's heard of. Your booking agent gets paid only when he / she successfully books you. Their ability to do so is hindered if you are virtually unheard of. Since this is how the agents get paid, they will only take you on if they feel there's reason to believe they can book you.

The way to obtain a booking agent is to play the numbers game. Send a press kit to as many booking agencies as you can locate. Once again you are trying to sell yourself, do your homework and make sure your press kit is well put together and professional.

If you are going to attempt to book your own independent tour it's important that you have built up or generated a "story"/buzz around your release. Some degree of college radio airplay, press, local chart activity or other notoriety so that you can interest venue owners in your act. You should begin generating this interest at least two or three months prior to launching any tour. After you've done a radio mail-out, concentrate on the stations that played your record or markets where you seem to be hot. Make sure your distributor is aware of these developments as well as your plans to tour. It's a good bet you are already building a fan base in these areas. Whenever possible, work with the local stations in trying to secure bookings. They know everything about the music scene in their town, most of them sponsor or present shows on campus or in town, and they have the clout to get the shows booked.

Getting the support of individual college and public stations is the best way to plan a tour. At the least, they can tell you what clubs in their city cater to your style of music. Ask if they would like to sponsor or in some way support the shows. Such a commitment from radio will no doubt include announcing the show on the air, giving away tickets to the show and doing an on-air interview with your band, not to mention increased airplay. If they're interested, call the area venues and tell them that your band is in the Top 10 at the local station, and that the station will be involved in the show.

Most venue owners won't agree to pay an out-of-town, independent band more than $750 to $1,000 for a full set, and you must demonstrate sufficiently that your performance will draw a substantial number of patrons. Quite often venue owners will not grant you a flat stated rate guarantee. They may prefer to pay you a percentage of the money collected at the door on the night of your performance. You should always try to get a flat guarantee or a combination of guarantee and percentage of the door. Always verify that the venue will be assisting in promoting the show, either in print media, local TV, radio or at least at the venue itself in the weeks leading up to the show.

SHOW SALES
As an independent label or artist you will not want to squander any opportunity to sell units and clearly there are few opportunities as prevalent as during a show. However, be careful, if you have product at retail through distribution you may be working against yourself. Attendees at your show may be hot to buy your product after hearing the live performance, but for each unit you sell at the show that is one less you will sell at retail POS. The reason this can be critical is that CDs sold at the venue are not receiving Soundscan credit, they're not counting at all. This will hurt your attempts to secure a major label or distribution deal. Always check with your distributor to make sure that product will be in the market by show time. If not, than go ahead and do what you have to do. When distribution is involved and in place the best way to ensure that your live performances generate sales is to work the crowd. You should ALWAYS pass out POP at the venue; it is a true blunder to not have

emblazoned on all your materials the phrase "In Stores NOW!" You can even go a step further and indicate which retailers are carrying your release, and don't be shy about saying the same thing on the microphone, more than once.

FAN CLUBS

If you have a mailing list of fans and friends, you can mail them catalogs or postcards that announce your new record and tell them where to pick it up. Live performances are a great time to add folks to your mailing list or fan club. If you don't have a mailing list, you should probably start one. A computer comes in handy here, but you can also write or type the addresses onto a piece of paper and photocopy this onto adhesive label stock that you can get at any stationery store. At venues you can have attendees sign a guest book, perhaps leaving their email addresses. If you have a computer you should put together an email mailing list (*see the Internet chapter [8] for more info*). Obtain mailing lists from others, get subscriber lists from magazines. Word of mouth is still the number one method of promotion, fan clubs are wonderful tools in that regard. As time goes on you will notice more and more attendees at your performances, it is ultimately how bands become famous and how CDs get sold.

VIDEO

The promotion of music releases is now synonymous with visualization or any sort of television related music programming. Such programming by means of conventional TV, cable, pay-cable, and direct satellite is powerful in its application as a promotional tool. Record labels learned years ago that sales could be enhanced in this manner of promotion. The concept is certainly not new, whether the forum was a movie musical, or a TV broadcast like the Beatles first US television appearance on the Ed Sullivan Show. Although the major labels still have their artists doing the talk show and variety show circuits, the method of choice in today's Music Industry is the music video and has been since the 1980s. Through the 1990s music video presentation became rife with highly technical productions, some with enormous budgets due to remote locations, extravagant sets and sophisticated special effects.

The Industry increased it's video production in the mid 1980s, particularly in an effort to stimulate sales of rock recordings. Rock fans took to them enthusiastically when MTV and its imitators increased exposure to video via cable TV. Now network and cable broadcast companies transmit dozens of video shows, both national and regional and the impact on record sales is profound. Videos can not only increase record sales, in some cases they can be wholly attributed with breaking new acts, even enhancing the chart life and shelf life of new releases.

Record labels today, already burdened with trying to influence radio playlists, hire promotion firms that are busier than ever trying to get their videos produced and aired in the marketplace. Though MTV is still the crown jewel of video promotion, promoters attack similar programming forums on the regional levels as well because they have substantial exposure in the region. Just as with commercial radio, MTV may prove too much to bite off initially, this is why promoters and labels aggressively market new video releases to secondary markets or regional networks for video exposure thus building a story around the releases with which to approach MTV and it's national counterparts.

MAILING CAMPAIGN FOLLOW-UPS
Promoters mail free promotional copies of new releases to a large number and variety of destinations. Mailing out this many free recordings is costly. Experienced promoters use a very select mailing list, one that includes mostly influential stations or stations where the promoter has personal contacts, and trades where they are fairly confident of receiving a review. Basically, destinations where the material is likely to be well received and where it is beneficial to send.

ALL Mail campaigns must be followed up by telephone calls. The success of this kind of telephone follow-up depends, not only on the suitability of the recordings mailed with respect to the destination, but the rapport between the caller and the recipient. If you are planning to hire an independent promotions firm to do either your mailing or the follow-up campaign, or both, you want to find a firm that has experience and very strong contacts and resources in the Industry. Don't be shy about asking them to facilitate some sort of confirmation or verification of the stated resources. Do your homework.

CLUB PROMOTION

Dance clubs have historically and consistently been effective places to measure the pulse of the 18 to 26 years of age music buying demographic. They are for that reason, great forums to test new music product. Prior to commercial release for retail consumption, record labels should look to test market their new product by launching a club promotion campaign. Send promotional copies of your pending release to appropriately formatted clubs. Whenever possible, this campaign should also include live performance bookings at clubs. Don't be shy about enlisting the aide of the DJs or club managers to help gauge response to your music. If the clubs report strong response, this could be a precursor to having a truly marketable release on your hands. Always be sure to share this information with your distributor, include it in your press kit for reviewers and radio. This particular type of campaign will not be cheap, most club DJs demand vinyl, sometimes two pieces each.

Most record labels supply clubs through record / DJ "pools". Servicing record pools is a good move, even critical for certain genres. If strong word of mouth develops through the network, and the track gains good airplay in that region, the single may be headed for the charts. Another way dance clubs contribute to record promotion is by showing music videos of new releases on high-resolution monitors or TVs in the club. Clubs obtain most of their tapes through video distribution companies that act as liaisons between record companies and the clubs. Dancers are literally surrounded by imagery and sensory intake with club's multiple screens and overpowering sound systems.

These same club-goers may be stimulated enough to later walk into a store and pick up a copy of your release to continue enjoying the vibe at home.

CAMPAIGN MANAGEMENT

In order to ensure efficiency and results, any promotional campaign must be tightly managed. With so many elements involved and so much follow up required, diligent management and oversight is a requisite. Whether you take this task on yourself or contract it out, it must be done. Many labels opting to self-mange their promotional campaigns will assign one particular individual to manage it. This is a good idea. That person will likely require assistance, however there should only be one person charged with oversight. The campaign manager should be aware of the budget he / she has to work with and should conduct the campaign in conjunction with the distributor. A good campaign manager will have a considerable awareness of market, regional and national data pertinent to your release and be able to conduct analysis of that data to derive sound strategy for the campaign. It cannot be stated enough how critical it is for the campaign manager to be in continuos contact with your distributor regarding all aspects and developments of the campaign. The manager will have the responsibility of assigning particular promotions personnel to certain geographic areas and to coordinate the efforts of staff promoters working in many different directions. If the distributor is unaware of such activity geographically, you run the risk of generating substantial consumer demand in a market or region and not have any units in stores there. This is actually a worse scenario than not promoting at all. Consumers eager to purchase your release may become disinterested if the title is not available to them at retail. Additionally, radio stations playing your track may cease doing so if the release is not available for their listeners to purchase. Proper, sound, management will ensure that this and other promotion blunders never occur.

With radio promotion campaigns in particular the campaign manager is sometimes called a "tracker"

89

because the job's primary responsibilities center around keeping track of which stations are adding or dropping the new release as well as spin rate or level of rotation. If the tracker observes good airplay developing in a particular geographic area, he / she may double efforts there in an attempt to develop a regional hit. If a regional breakout occurs, it can, if properly managed, be parlayed into a national hit.

The tracking person or manager also has the task of following the progress of a new release on the trade charts. The early rise and fall of a recording on the charts provides guidance on how to spend (*or withdraw*) the money available for a particular campaign.

ADVERTISING

Advertising is obviously an important component of music promotion campaigns. A wide variety of media have proven effective, such as print, broadcast, point-of-sale, and direct mail. All advertising seems to help sales in a general sense, but the difficulty is measuring whether the resulting sales justify the expense. Do not allow sentiment (or for example, your desire to see your release on television), to play a part, base it solely on the numbers. Different advertising media will show results differently and along different timelines. For example: if your monitoring your sales as a measure, a print media ad schedule will take more time to manifest sales than a weekend blitz radio schedule. Be patient when required but be decisive and proactive when necessary.

Advertising can be cooperative, with the label and the store sharing costs, or institutional; for example, a print page or media buy, that mentions a store or particular retailer. Co-op advertising may be paid up front, all or in part by the retailer or the distributor, then reimbursed by the label from a co-op budget determined by the retailer's volume of purchases from the distributor. To justify the high expense, several titles are pushed in one ad, thus pulling down the "cost-per-thousand" expense per title. Local record store chains will frequently place print ads in newspapers. However, the record label may in fact pay for all, or part of the costs for such ads. Sometimes record stores request that record labels finance a print media campaign in their area through the distributor. Or, the label itself initiates print ads, particularly when it is trying to coordinate advertising with the promotion of local concerts.

CHAPTER 11

The Art of Marketing and Promotion in Today's Music Industry

"If business is war, and I truly believe that it is; then structured marketing campaigns are the stratagems by which wars are won." - **Dameon V. Russell**

Welcome to my world! This is where it all happens, MARKETING and PROMOTION. It is here in the trenches where destinies are realized, where it is determined whether music titles live or die. This is the part of the Industry you must have true love for in order to succeed. What you will hopefully come away with after reading this chapter is an accurate understanding of what must transpire to achieve success and retail sales of your music product release. I shall endeavor to relay to you aspects of music marketing and promotion that are vital to that success; i.e. retail promotion, radio promotion, generating consumer demand, distribution of promotional materials and much more. If success is your ultimate objective and marketing is perhaps in your blood a bit, you will be excited and motivated by the lessons and knowledge contained within this chapter. What you will not be, either way, is bored!

It's ironic, as much of my Industry related career, my life, has been devoted to marketing and promotion, I have no recollection of ever looking up the word "marketing" in Webster's. Not to worry, I have my own definition which is, I think more directly appropriate to the Music Industry. I'll quote myself here. Marketing:

"The propagation of a given product or consumable upon an otherwise unaware consumer group via creative and targeted messaging." – **Dameon V. Russell**

Listen, that's it in a nutshell. I'm not certain how Webster's defines the word but that has got to be close. Marketing is the term best used to describe a very general task. I say general only because in that sense it refers to all industries, just about any product must be marketed in some way, shape or form. In this regard the Music Industry does not differ. However, close comparison will reveal differences in how we market in this industry as opposed to how the task is approached in others.

Falling back on my aforementioned definition of the task, that's pretty much the sum of it irrespective of what you are marketing. Where we differ primarily in the Music Industry is in the tools at our disposal. I am not really comfortable stating it in that context, ".... at our disposal" because that implies choice or free will in the selection of what tools you would utilize and which ones you would not. This is simply not accurate. The tools involved in the marketing of music product such as radio, live performance, retail, etc. MUST each be exercised in every campaign; there is no choice in that. Not doing so, and not understanding the often subtle correlation between these and all the elements of a properly structured music marketing campaign is to fail in the execution of such.

Additional elements specific to music marketing include the understanding of life span / shelf life, genre, radio format. Of course not all of these are exclusive to music product, but they are more pertinent in music marketing. Going back to what I stated in the previous paragraph about the often-subtle relationship between all campaign elements. In no other industry perhaps is this more essential to understand. One, two or even three without the fourth is failure, period. Take for instance the mechanics of the combustible engine. If all cylinders are not firing in that well choreographed symphony you have a skip or a miss which ultimately causes among other things, loss of power. In music marketing, that miss is fatal to your product release. What good does it do to have a band gigging at venues throughout a given market if there is no product at retail in that market? Where is the benefit in having product pressed and retail ready if you are

93

not engaged in retail promotion to get the Buyer's and Retail Account Reps to place your product in their outlets? How are you helping to generate retail sales in Columbia, Ohio if your band is only gigging in Boston? "D", the answer to all of the above is, you are not! No more than if you are engaged in street promotions throughout San Francisco but have no product placed within that market.

Please understand, I only know of one true objective in this Industry, which is to sell product. So sure, if you are diligently engaged in any of the promotional activities above, you ARE marketing. Cool. But to what end, popularity, name recognition? Those are but mere side effects, certainly not worthy objectives. What I am trying to impress upon you is the critical nature of timing, relation and symbiosis that must be factored into every music marketing campaign involving all elements of that campaign in order to bring about the possibility of success for that campaign.

IDENTIFYING AND TARGETING

Ever hear the proverb "knowledge is power"? In order to effectively market music product, you better learn first to truly appreciate this phrase. I hope you have realized by now that this chapter, indeed this book is in general terms, written from the Indie perspective. Major label campaigns differ in methodology from that of the Indie band or Label. Major Labels are afforded the luxury of that difference in methodology thanks to their overwhelming capital reserve which facilitates enormous marketing and promotion budgets. Let's remain firmly planted here, as Indies, we must.

If you have ever had the benefit of marketing 101 then you should be familiar with the two general types of marketing. Those are targeted marketing and guerrilla marketing. Applied to music marketing both are effective, only one is efficient; can you guess which one? Good answer, I hope. Targeted marketing. The Majors' methodology is that of the guerrilla marketer. Sure there is some specificity involved; I'm sure you would not catch an N'Sync video on the Country video channel CMC. However, for the most part the Majors are spending vast sums of money to reach a specific consumer demographic by propagating the message, well, just about everywhere. Hey, they can afford to do so, selectively. I'm assuming that you can not. Targeted marketing is much more efficient, though trickier as well; at the end of the day, targeted marketing is much more effective.

Now, to tailor a marketing plan to a very specific consumer means that you must first identify that consumer. When discussing targeting there is one word most relevant and that is, specificity. I not only refer to specifically identifying who the consumer is, but also where they are and what they are. Remember that knowledge is power. The power to effectively and efficiently market your release. I call it **D.P.G.H.** analysis.

Demographics — the consumer "what's"
Psychographics — the consumer "who's"
Geographic — the consumer "where's"
Historical data — historical sales analysis

It has been my overwhelming experience that if you follow this path, you will find yourself at the front door of your targeted consumer. The way this works is to develop an understanding of these four elements as they apply to your targeted consumer. Doing so will enable you to design a most creative and direct approach to reach these consumers specifically.

The term demographics may be familiar to you, most marketers like to collectively refer to the sum of D.P.G.H. as demographics, and I do not subscribe that philosophy. It has been my experience that the more specific your approach to analysis, the more specifically you will be able to define, target and reach your consumer. Make no mistake; D.P.G.H. was born wholly of my experience. In fact, I don't even think "psychographics" is an English language word but it is, if only subtly, different than demographics. In my methodology demographics is the understanding of

95

what the consumers are. What age, race, gender, etc. Psychograhics is an extension of the "what's" that I use to tell me more specifically who the consumer is; a better understanding of what their tendencies are, what trends they follow, almost what their mentality is. An example: teen consumers in the suburbs of Oakland, CA will certainly mirror demographically teen consumers in rural Kansas but psychographically, they are worlds apart. If you were attempting to identify, target and reach this demographic to market a talented white rapper like Da Professor or Eminem, this psychographic data would be of great benefit; you think?

Geographical data is pretty straightforward and as you can see from the example in the previous paragraph, it is relative to the total analysis and understanding of your consumer. Sure, people from different parts of the world are as individual per their locale as fingerprints for the most part. Well domestically this is also the case. In fact, within a single given market, people can be just as individual based on their geographic locale within that market; i.e. suburbs, inner city, rural, north, east, west or south side.

Even if you are marketing an Artist's debut effort, analysis of historical sales data is relevant and important. Obviously if it's a debut release, there is no prior sales history for that Artist. However, understanding the prior sales history of other releases, in that same market, of Artists or bands of the same genre will benefit you greatly. If you are taking a look at Birmingham, AL because you are considering spending marketing dollars there to promote a Ska band, you might be interested to know how well the band No Doubt sold in Birmingham.

The purpose of all this data analysis is to apply it in your efforts to derive consumer appropriate marketing stratagems involving a myriad of weapons such as radio, college campuses, street promotions, servicing of DJ pools, etc. As I stated, specificity is king and if you follow the road signs along the way, you will inevitably arrive at the front doors of consumers more likely to purchase your music.

RETAIL PROMOTION

You should consider yourself ahead of the field, just a bit, if you know precisely what retail promotion is. Many people do not and many who think they do, often have it misunderstood. If you are fortunate enough to have landed any sort of mainstream distribution deal or if you are currently exploring distribution firms, be certain to inquire about the level of retail promotion they will do on behalf of your title. You may have to contract a firm independent of your distributor to handle retail promotions on your behalf. Retail promoters push your product title to retail Buyers and Account Reps in order to get them to "buy-in" or place your product on the shelves of their P.O.S. (*point of sale*) outlets.

Retail sales are not guaranteed, that much you know. Well neither is placement at retail. It is important to understand that this is a two-sale game. Before you can sell product to the end user, the consumer, you must first sell your product to the individuals charged with the responsibility of determining what product gets placement in the stores. Retail Buyers and Account Reps. Clearly if you are unsuccessful making the first sale the second is moot.

A distributor typically does not possess the manpower to individually promote all the titles in their catalog. Their catalog is distributed to and reviewed by the Buyers and hey, you are in the book right. Well the problem is one of diligence really. Buyers should conduct diligence, thoroughly researching things like airplay, performance schedules, promotion activities, etc. For all of those titles? No way. A good retail promoter details this type of vital information relative to your band and communicates such directly to the Buyers and Reps helping them make good and warranted product placement decisions for your release. In essence they lift your release off the pages and out of the clutter of the sea of releases facing the Buyers. Retail promoters will need to be constantly aware of your performance schedule, where you are conducting street promotions, any radio play you may be getting, etc. Recall if you will my statements earlier regarding the correlation of multiple elements and how essential that is. If you will be in Indianapolis next month for a series of gigs at various venues, imagine the missed opportunity if you were to not have any product in retail outlets anywhere in Indianapolis.

Co-op deals or promotions with retail are great tools and are one of the things a good retail promoter will endeavor to set up on your behalf. A retail co-op deal is basically as it sounds. In exchange for a fee, particular retailers will buy-in a predetermined amount of units (*your CD*) for a predetermined quantity of their outlets. These deals are generally regional in scope. Let's take that hypothetical Indianapolis scenario; say your retail promoter was able to structure a co-op with Best Buy on your behalf in conjunction with that series of scheduled performances. Best Buy would buy-in enough units to cover their twelve Indianapolis outlets with perhaps ten units each. You may also have radio ad schedules attached promoting your gigs or maybe print advertising in the market both also promoting the fact that your CD is available for purchase at Best Buy. You then print your promotional materials just as you would to pass out at any live performance only this time you include on your posters or flyers that your CD is in stores now and readily available at Best Buy. Co-ops are a fantastic way to get your product placed in major point of sale outlets, develop awareness and relationships with major retailers, and of course, sell CDs!

Just a note, even if you are still on the path of consignment in a local / small market, you can work out these types of co-op structures with retailers at the in-store management level. Most likely with the same individual that agreed to let your product in on consignment basis.

RADIO PROMOTION

Radio promotion is wrought with many, many myths. No better way to begin this discussion than to dispel at least some of those myths. The biggest one I think is that, if you get radio play on one station, or in one market, it will just spread to other stations like a wild fire or the mythological domino effect. Not! Another more notable myth about radio is that Major label artists automatically get rotation at commercial radio. Not! How about the one where knowing a DJ or on-air personality can get you rotation? Not! Listen, none of these statements is at all true. The fact is that every song you hear magically in rotation at commercial radio is the result of a well planned, well executed arduous radio promotion campaign that typically began at non-commercial radio. The objective of any radio promotion campaign is to accrue "adds" (*when a station adds your track to their play list*) at commercial regular rotation radio and to subsequently chart. There are different types of radio, for the sake of simplicity you should concern yourself with only two forms of radio. They are non-commercial, and commercial.

Non-commercial radio or non-comm. can be further broken down into three segments, community radio, NPR (*National Public Radio*) and of course, College radio. Particularly for Indies initiating a radio promotion campaign, non-comm. radio is where you want to begin, specifically College radio. * There are about 1,000 college radio stations in the U.S. and Canada, of these Alternative music comprises 75% of all the music at these stations.

Alternative or not, College radio represents the absolute fast track for getting airplay. Getting "adds" is still the objective, however unlike commercial radio, getting an add at non-comm. means being added to that stations library of music, not necessarily to the play list. The underlying objective is still the same, accrue adds and hit the charts. CMJ (*College Music Journal*) is about the most respected non-comm. radio play tracking chart vehicle. It is also in my opinion the best industry resource for seeing or taking notice of new music. Many College radio stations report their air play data to CMJ which then utilizes that data to develop / determine its charts. CMJ has several different charts therein increasing even further your chances of hitting one of them. In a good radio promotion the objective is to obtain adds at College radio, break onto one of the CMJ charts thus creating what we call a story for your title, then leverage that story to begin your assault on commercial radio. You must begin this way, to think that you can break commercial radio ranks with no story and no (*recent*) history of airplay at non-comm. is simply nonsense.

Commercial regular-rotation, what a trip. It's been said that if precious metals and gems such as diamonds and gold were as abundantly available as, say, boy bands, they would be as inexpensive as your daily newspaper; or something like that. The fact is that the rarity of these commodities is what makes them so valuable. Well, that's commercial regular-rotation radio, your single spinning anywhere from nine to twenty-five times or more per week at a given station; the crown jewel of any radio promotion campaign.

Commercial radio is certainly a difficult nut to crack, and in terms of independent radio promotion firms it's quite an expensive campaign to mount. If you are talking to DJs you are wasting your breath. DJs no more determine what gets airplay than a MacDonald's employee determines what's going to be on the menu. You must understand that the average commercial station is owned by a corporate parent, generally a large broadcasting company; i.e. Clear Channel, Cox, Radio One, Cumulus, Infinity, etc. You must understand also, and I'm only going to say this once because it's been known to hurt some people, radio stations are NOT in the music business. They are in the advertisement or air time business. A station's programming is the key component in determining the volume of revenue brought in by the sales force. Why? Because the programming reels in listeners and that determines ratings, which in turn dictates what the station can charge the pool of advertisers in their market for ad schedules. No different than network television. Why is it that a thirty-second spot during the Super Bowl can fetch a million dollars? Because "Neilson" says there are millions of people watching!

In determining whether or not a song gets added, the Program Director must weigh whether or not doing so will retain the precious listeners the station already has or even if it may garner new ones. Believe me, Program Directors are in a tenuous position. Crafting a play list

Source: Bryan Farrish - "Radio Airplay 101"

that results in a falling market share and a decrease in ad revenue is a certain path to unemployment.

View commercial radio as a giant and your assault on that giant should begin at the knees. Identify first, smaller stations or ones in smaller / secondary markets. Remember, conquering smaller stations or ones in secondary markets is not automatically going to net you large market commercial stations through the mythical ripple effect. But building a story for yourself in these smaller markets and stations can be used to leverage airplay in the larger markets as your campaign continues. Remember also that charting is a product of spin count; achieve enough adds at commercial regular-rotation and you just may realize national chart entry on Radio & Records (R&R) for instance.

Generally speaking, non-comm. radio does not sell CDs, at least not substantial quantities, that ultimate objective is only truly realized through commercial regular-rotation radio play. I simply can not stress enough that merely sending your single to radio, non-comm. or commercial, is NOT radio promotion. True radio promotion takes six to eight weeks of calling, faxing or emailing each station after you have mailed your CD in. This is referred to as tracking and rotation is not going to be achieved without it; often times not even for the Majors but certainly never for the Indie.

Although you can assume the task of tracking yourself, it is more often something you would hire a professional radio promotion firm to handle on your behalf. The best in the business at "working" your record to radio in my experience is Bryan Farrish Radio Promotions of Southern California. If you do choose to work the record yourself, start by identifying non-comm. and commercial stations in your strong markets or markets in line with the rest of your marketing plan. You will need to research addresses, telephone and fax numbers as well as the name of the Music Director or Program Director for each of the stations on your list. Send your music in a professionally presented package. Package should include a radio edit single professionally manufactured only, in a standard jewel case with song and artist clearly printed on both spines. You may want to include a One Sheet and any current radio airplay data you already have. Also a performance schedule if you are gigging in their market. Shortly after you have completed the mailing, make contact with each station to make the Music Director or Program Director aware that the new music package is coming. Do this and you increase the likelihood that your package will be opened and reviewed. Let them know you will give them a call next week just to confirm that they received it. Then, you got it, next week your six to eight week campaign begins! Be sure to take very detailed notes of your telephone communications, even if you just leave a message make note of that. That may be a station you should fax or email that week.

The most important thing you are trying to convey in communicating with the station programmers is that a story is building around your material in their market; i.e. sales, press, other radio stations, interviews sold out or packed live performances, etc. You can get frustrated, it's allowed; just don't ever give up!

STREET PROMOTION

All other elements considered, there still is no better way to generate consumer awareness than creating a buzz on the street through relentless and ever present street promotion. You Marketing 101 grads know this to be true. You have learned that despite today's multi-million dollar ad campaign budgets and sixty second television commercials that run more like mini motion pictures; the number one method of advertising and still Heavyweight Champion of the ad world is, word of mouth!

Street promotion has many forms; from live performance to passing out printed promotional materials, and everything in between. As with all the other elements of music marketing campaigns previously discussed, your street promotions must be managed or staged in an organized, systematic fashion. Timing, as always, is critical. The objective is to create that aforementioned buzz at the street level, the rules, well there are none! You want to distribute as much material in as many relevant locations as possible.

Recall now your D.P.G.H. data analysis, do you remember finding yourself at the front door of your targeted consumer? Well, you didn't conduct that diligence because you are a stalker, I hope. You did so because you have a message to relay to them. Now that you have found them in their domain, whether that be the malls, homes, clubs, high schools, churches or happy hour in the financial district downtown, you must get your message conveyed. Let me shed light on some of the more common tools of conveyance. Any worthy street campaign will include the following:

• Posters (*11 x 17 or larger*)
• Postcards (*double sided if you can swing it*)
• Snippet CDs (*each of the tracks of your album minimized to around 1:30 / teaser*)
• Promotional copies of the full album or your chosen radio single
• Vinyl (*if you can swing it – it's not cheap but many club & radio DJs prefer it*)
• Flyers (*preferably with local performance date info.*)

These are the basic, minimal tools of conveyance for

every street campaign. If you have a more than moderate budget, there are of course greater lengths you can go to. I hate to be stereotypical, but if you are in a rock band, I know you have a gig van; right? A vehicle wrap will cost you anywhere from $1,500 to $3,000. This is a where a mural like design is crafted by artisans and is applied thoroughly covering your vehicle essentially turning it into a rolling billboard; very effective. You also have the option of hiring a street team; a firm that will take your promotional tools and saturate any given market. Street teams can be very costly depending upon the scope of the territory you want them to cover. Great for markets not local to you and therefore could not be work effectively by you. That is also the number one drawback concerning street teams; you are not there, how can you know how diligently they are working the territory for your money? The best guard against bogus street teams is to thoroughly investigate them before hiring them. Make sure you check their references completely. The best result with street teams is usually achieved when personally referred to you by someone you trust, perhaps another band or artist of your same genre. Cash is king as they say, there are many alternatives available for you to use in a street campaign if you are working with a sizable budget. Bus bench advertising is effective, merchandising as well: (*coffee mugs, match books, calendars, T-shirts, hats, mouse pads, buttons, bumper stickers, license plate frames, text book covers, print advertisements, contests and giveaways, etc.*).

Greater lengths aside, you can mount a successful street campaign with the basic tools of conveyance. The absolute most significant tool at your disposal is not shown on the list because it deserves it's own space on the marketing mantle; that is live performance! There is nothing more effective. If you are not rehearsing a stage show and gigging at least in your own market, you are not doing your job. Managers, if you have bands / artists sitting at home calling you everyday to ask how sales are looking, your clients need a new manager! Artists must

104

perform; as often and for the benefit of as many persons as possible. Some of the most egregious faux pas made in music marketing happen in the street campaigns.   When performing, it is a monstrous blunder to not have large quantities of your printed materials to distribute to patrons in attendance. If you have distribution, even if it's just local consignment, the absolute largest oversight (*actually quite common too*) is to distribute printed materials that do not let people know that the CD is in stores and in which ones. You may scratch your head at the thought of bands and management making these terrible oversights, but they are more common than you would dare to imagine.

THE SUM OF IT ALL

Well, you would want the sum of it to be record sales. Never fool yourself into believing that this game is about anything else.   Some may say that's terribly shallow or even cynical. Some may believe it to be contemporary or just realistic. Whatever you believe, know this; this is the Music BUSINESS. Business is the operative word and with multi-billion dollar annual revenues; its players are not non-profit businesses. As I stated in my opening, marketing and promotion is where the Business of Music transpires. As a Label, Artist, Manager or Distributor the efforts you make and the campaigns you wage in this regard will be the most decisive or influential aspects of any success you hope to achieve.

I delight in marketing and promotion; I am passionate about it. In no other area of business is the "reward for work" ratio so justifiably substantial. Your results are tangible here; you work the album hard, determine, via very specific demographic analysis, to whom it should be worked. You guide, manipulate, adapt, and execute your marketing plan from a bird's eye view of all elements like a well-contrived battle plan. Success is measurable by the most gratifying standard of all, record sales; and the dividends are paid of the most welcome currency of all, cash!

You need not share my enthusiasm for marketing, just

understand the vital nature of it. Understand all of the variables and elements involved. Know that the correlation and relationship between them all is what ultimately determines your level of success. Work your album because you know that people deserve to hear your music. Yes, the Music Industry is abundant with fulfilled dreams and satisfied dreamers, but accept that it is through sound, diligent marketing and promotion that those dreams were realized; and it is only in this manner that your dreams will be as well. GOOD LUCK!

APPENDIX: 1

Performing rights organizations monitor radio, television, motion Pictures and events and collect royalties, which you'll receive a share of if you are a member and your music gets played in any of these media. The two major companies in the United States are ASCAP and BMI.

USA

ASCAP
One Lincoln Plaza
New York, NY 10023
212-621-6000

PO Box 11171
Chicago, ILL 60611
312-481-1194

7920 Sunset Blvd. #300
Los Angeles, CA 90046
213-883-1000

2 Music Square W.
Nashville, TN 37203
615-742-5000

52 Haymaker
Stes. 10 & 11
London SW1 Y4RP
England
011 44 71 973 0069

BMI
320 West 57th St.
New York, NY 10019
212-586-2000

8730 Sunset Bl. 3rd. fl.
Los Angeles, CA 90069
310-659-9109

10 Music Square E.
Nashville, TN 37203
615-291-6700

AUSTRALIA

APRA
PO Box 567
Crows Nest NSW 2065
AUSTRAILA
(02) 922-6422

EUROPE

PRS
29-33 Berners Street
London W1P 4AA
England
(071)580-5544

SESAC
421 W. 54th
New York, NY 10019
212-586-3450

55 Music Square E.
Nashville, TN 37203
615-320-0055

CANADA

SOCAN
1201 West Pendor #400
Vancouver BC V6E 2V2
Canada
604-669-5569

600 Blvd. De Maisonneve West
Suite 500
Montreal PQ H3A 312
Canada
514-844-8377

41 Valleybrook Dr.
Don Mills ONT M3B 2S6
Canada
416-445-8700

<u>TRADE PUBLICATIONS</u>

Album Network
120 N.Victory Blvd. 3rd fl.
Burbank, CA 91502
818-955-4000

(Retail and Radio Charts for Rock and Alternative Rock.
Published weekly,300-reporters. Also publishes
"Yellow Pages of Rock" directory, yearly)

Billboard
1515 Broadway
New York, NY 10036
800- 669-1002

(Radio and Retail, over 1,000 reporters, All musical
styles, including classical. Published-weekly)

Radio and Records (R&R)
1930 Century Park West
Los Angeles, CA 90067
213-553-4330

(Charts by format: Contemporary Hit Radio, Adult
Contemporary, Jazz, New Age, Album Oriented Rock,
Country, New Rock. 1,000-reporters, published-weekly)

CMJ New Music Report
245 Great Neck Road, 3rd fl.
Great Neck, NY 11021
516-466-6000

(Majority of stations listed are college. Over 1,000 stations
and retailers report weekly. Rock, Rap, Reggae, World
Music, Metal, Jazz, Alternative. CMJ puts on yearly
CMJ Music Marathon in NYC that features showcases
Of emerging bands)

The Hard Report
4 Trading Post Way
Medford Lakes, NJ 08055
609-654-7272

(Radio Charts for AOR, Alternative, Metal. Over 250
reporters, interviews, music news, new releases.
Published-weekly)

Hits
14958 Ventura Blvd.
Sherman Oaks, CA 91403
818-501-7900
(Radio and Retail Charts, over 700-radio station
reporters. Published-weekly)

Net
22 E. 21st St.
New York, NY 10010
212-420-0717

(College Radio, Club, Retail Charts. Includes
feature articles, reviews and more. Published-monthly,
weekly fax charts also available. Also runs alternative
and dance music record pools)

COLLEGE RADIO STATIONS

This list is derived from College Stations through-out the United States and Canada that have a strong frequency and substantial power. (10,000 to 100,000 Watts). There are around 900 US and Canadian college radio stations, however the focus of this list is a larger broadcast radius due to the amount of frequency and wattage.

CANADA

CISM
C.P. 6128 Succ. A
Montreal Quebec
Canada H3C 317
(514) 343-7511
89.3 FM
10,000 Watts
ALL

CHUO
University of Ottawa
85 University Street
Student Federation
Ottawa, ONT
Canada K1N 6N5
(613) 564-2903
89.1 FM
18,200 Watts
ALL

CKCU
Carleton University
University Center Rm. 517
Ottawa, ONT
Canada K1S 5B6
(613) 788-2898
(613) 788-4060 fax
93.1 FM
12,000 Watts
ALL

CILQ
2 Bloor Street, Suite 3000
Toronto, ONT
Canada M4W 1A8
(416) 967-3445
(416) 924-2479 fax
107.1 FM
100,000 Watts
Rock

CFNY
1 Younge Street, 25th Floor
Toronto, ONT
Canada M5E 1G1
(416) 453-7542
(416) 453-7711 fax
102.1 FM
40,000 Watts
Alt.

UNITED STATES

ALASKA

KBBI
Kachemak Bay
Broadcasting, Inc.
3913 Kachemak Wy.
Homer, AK 99603
(907) 235-7721
(907) 235-2357 fax
890 AM
10,000 Watts
ALL

ARIZONA

KUPD
1900 W. Carmen
Tempe, AZ 85283
(602) 838-0400
(602) 820-8469 fax
98.7 FM
100,000 Watts
Rock

ARKANSAS

KABF
1501 Arch Street
Little Rock, AR 72202
(501) 372-6119
88.3 FM
100,000 Watts
ALL

KMJX
11101 Anderson Dr.
Little Rock, AR 72212
(501) 372-6598
105.1 FM
79,000 Watts
Classic Rock

CALIFORNIA

KROQ
PO Box 10670
Burbank, CA 91505
(818) 567-1067
(818) 520-1329 fax
106.7 FM
50,000 Watts
Com. Alt

91X-FM
XTRA

4891 Pacific Coast Hwy
San Diego, CA 92110
(619) 294-2916
91.1 FM
100,000 Watts
Com. Alt.

KTYD
PO Box 62110
Santa Barbara, CA 93160
(805) 967-4511
(805) 964-4430 fax
99.9 FM
34,000 Watts
AOR

KXJZ
3416 American River Dr. Suite B
Sacramento, CA 95864
(916) 485-5977
90.9 FM
50,000 Watts
Jazz

COLORADO

KCSU
Colorado State University
Lory Student Center
Fort Collins, CO 80523
(303) 491-7611
90.5 FM
10,000 Watts
ALL

KTSC
University of Southern Colorado
2200 Bonforte Blvd.
Pueblo, CO 81001
(719) 549-2822
89.5 FM
10,000 Watts
AOR

CONNECTICUT

WPKN
University of
Bridgeport
244 University Ave.
Bridgeport, CT 06601
(203) 576-4895
89.5 FM
10,000 Watts
Jazz,Classical, Urban,
Exp.

FLORIDA

WKGC
Gulf Coast Community
College
5230 West Hwy 98
Panama City, FL 32401
(904) 769-5242
(904) 872-3836 fax
90.7 FM
100,000 Watts
ALL

WDRK
8813 Thomas Dr.
Panama City Beach, FL
32408
(904) 235-1061
105.9 FM
56,000 Watts
Alt.

WMNF
1210 E. Martin Luther
King Jr.
Tampa, FL 33603
(813) 238-8001
(813) 237-4259 fax
88.5 FM
70,000 Watts

Jazz, Blues, New Age,
Reggae, Hip-Hop

WXTB
2 Corporate Dr. #550
Clearwater, FL 34622
(813) 572-9808
(813) 573-2994 fax
97.9 FM
100,000 Watts
Rock,Metal, Alt.

GEORGIA

WRAS
Georgia State University
University Center
Box 1813
Atlanta, GA 30302
(404) 651-2240
88.5 FM
100,000 Watts
Rap, Alt., Raggae, Folk

WUOG
University of Georgia
Box 2065
Memorial Hall
Athens, GA 30602
(706) 542-8466
(706) 542-0351 fax
90.5 FM
10,000 Watts
Alt., Blues, Country, Rap, Reggae

ILLINOIS

WBEZ
105 W. Adams, 39th fl.
Chicago, IL 60603
(312) 641-5196
(312) 641-6234 fax
91.5 FM
10,000 Watts
Jazz, World, Latin, Folk

WEFT
113 N. Market
Champaign, IL 61820
(217) 359-9338
90.1 FM
10,000 Watts
ALL

WVJC
Walbash Valley College
2200 College Dr.
Mt. Carmel, IL 62863
(618) 262-8989
89.1 FM
50,000 Watts
Rock, AOR

INDIANA

WAJC
Butler University
2835 North Illinois
Street
Indianapolis, IN 46208
(317) 926-9252
(317) 927-5971 fax
104.5 FM
48,000 Watts
Alt.

WISU
Indiana State
University
Room 107 Dreiser Hall
Terre Haute, IN 47809
(812) 237-3256
89.7 FM
25,000 Watts
ALL

IOWA

KFMG
108 Third Street, Suite

114

103
Des Moines, IA 50309
(515) 282-1033
103.3 FM
100,000 Watts
ALL

KUNI
University of Northern Iowa
Broadcasting Building, 3rd Fl.
Cedar Fall, IA 50614
(319) 273-6400
(319) 273-2682 fax
90.9 FM
100,000 Watts
ALL

KENTUCKY

WFPL
301 York Street
Louisville, KY 40203
(502) 561-8640
(502) 561-8640 fax
89.3 FM
100,000 Watts
Jazz, Blues, Folk, Bluegrass

WNKU
N. Kentucky University
Highland Heights, KY 41076
(606) 572-7897
89.7 FM
12,000 Watts
Adult Alt.

LOUISANA

KRVS
University
of Southwest Louisiana
PO Box 42171
Lafayette, LA 70504
(318) 231-5668

(318) 231-6101 fax
88.7 FM
100,000 Watts
ALL

MARYLAND

WHFS
8201 Corporate Dr.
Suite 550
Landover, MD 20785
(301) 306-0991
99.1 FM
50,000 Watts
Alt.

MASSACHUSETTS

WBCN
1265 Bolston Street
Boston, MA 02215
(617) 266-1111
104.1 FM
50,000 Watts
Rock, Alt.

MICHIGAN

WDET
WayneState University
6001 Cass Ave
Detroit, MI 48202
(313) 577-34146
(313) 577-1300 fax
101.9 FM
79,000 Watts
Alt.

CIMX
30100 Telegraph Rd.
Suite 262
Birmingham, MI 48232
(313) 961-9811
(313) 961-1603 fax

115

88.7 FM
100,000 Watts
Alt.

MINNESOTA

KJJO
11320 Valley View Rd.
Eden Prarie, MN 55344
(612) 941-5774
(612) 941-8750 fax
104.1 FM
100,000 Watts
Country

KMSU
Mankato State University
MSU Box 153
Mankato, MN 56002
89.7 FM
20,000 Watts

KVSC
St. Cloud Sate University
27 Stewart Hall
St. Cloud, MN 56301
(612) 255-3066
88.1 FM
16,500 Watts
ALL *except classical

MISSISSIPPI

WOKJ
1550 Tower Rd.
Bolten, MS 39041
1550 AM
50,000 Watts
ALL

WMXU
608 Yellow Jacket Dr.
Starkville, MS 39759
(601) 323-1230
(106.1 FM

50,000 Watts
Classic Rock

MISSOURI

KHTK
702 Moirkirk Ln
Manchester, MO 63011
97.1 FM
100,000 Watts
ALL

KDHX
3504 Magnolia
St. Louis, MO 63163
(314) 664-3955
(314) 849-1604 fax
88.1 FM
50,000 Watts
Rock, Blues,
Bluegrass, Ethnic

NEVADA

KUNV
University of
Nevada/Las Vegas
4505 S. Maryland
Pkwy
Las Vegas, NV 89154
(702) 739-3877
91.5 FM
15,000 Watts
ALL

NEW JERSEY

WBGO
54 Park Pl.
Newark, NJ 07102
(201) 624-8880
88.3 FM
10,000 Watts
Jazz

WPRB
Princeton University
Box 342
Princeton, NJ 08542
(609) 258-3655
103.3 FM
30,000 Watts
ALL

NEW MEXICO

KUNM
University of New Mexico
Campus & Girard NE
Albuquerque, NM 87131
(505) 277-8018
89.9 FM
13,600 Watts
Jazz, Rock, Folk, Blues

NEW YORK

WNEW
655 3rd Ave
New York, NY 10017
(212) 286-1027
(212) 599-5339 fax
102.7 FM
50,000 Watts
AOR

WFUV
Fordham University
Bronx, NY 10461
(718) 365-8050
(718) 365-9815 fax
90.7 FM
50,000 Watts
Alt.

WNYE
New York City Board of Education
112 Tillary Street
Brooklyn, NY 11201
(718) 935-4480

(718) 855-8863 fax
91.5 FM
20,000 Watts
Reggae, Rap, Country

WRPI
Renssalear Polytechnic
Institute
1 WRPI Plaza
Troy, NY 12180
(518) 276-6248
91.5 FM
10,000 Watts
Alt., Jazz, World

NORTH CAROLINA

WNCW
Isothermal Community
College
PO Box 804
Spindale, NC 28160
(704) 287-8000
(704) 286-1120 fax
88.7 FM
17,000 Watts
ALL *except classical

WXRC
PO Box 938
Hickory, NC 28601
95.7 FM
100,000 Watts
ALL

OHIO

WCBE
Columbus Public
Schools
540 Jack Gibbs Blvd.
Columbus, OH 43215
(614) 365-5555
90.5 FM

11,000 Watts
ALL

WZIP
University of Akron
Akron, OH 44325
(216) 972-8888
88.1 FM
33,000 Watts
Rap, Urban, Jazz

WVXU
Xavier University
38 Victoria Pkwy
Cincinnati, OH 45207
(513) 731-9898
(513) 745-3483 fax
91.7 FM
26,000 Watts
ALL

WYSO
Antioch College
Yellow Springs, OH 45387
(516) 767-6420
(516) 767-9422 fax
91.3 FM
10,000 Watts
ALL

OREGON

KBOO
20 SE 8th Ave
Portland, OR 97214
(503) 231-8032
90.7 FM
26,000 Watts
Rock, Blues

PENNSYLVANIA

WQSU
Susquehanna University
Selinsgrove, PA 17870

(717) 286-8400
88.9 FM
12,000 Watts
Rock

WVIA
70 Old Boston Rd.
Pittston, PA 18640
(717) 655-2808
(717) 655-1180 fax
89.9 FM
50,000 Watts
Classical, Folk, Jazz,
Alt., Rock

WMMR
19th & Walnut Street
Philadelphia, PA 19103
(215) 561-0933
93.3 FM
29,000 Watts
Rock, Alt., Classic
Rock

RHODE ISLAND

WHJY
115 Eastern Ave
E. Providence, RI
02914
(401) 438-6110
(401) 232-6312 fax
94.1 FM
50,000 Watts
AOR

TENNESSEE

WEVL
518 S. Main Street
Memphis, TN 38103
(901) 528-0560
89.9 FM

12,590 Watts
ALL

TEXAS

KDGE
1320 Greenway Dr.
700 Courtyard Tower
Irving, TX 75038
(214) 580-9400
(214) 580-9450 fax
94.5 FM
100,000 Watts
Alt., Rock

KERA
3000 Harry Hines Blvd.
Dallas, TX 75201
(214) 871-1390
(214) 754-0635 fax
90.1 FM
95,000 Watts
Folk, Jazz, Blues

KNON
PO Box 710909
Dallas, TX 75371
(214) 824-6893
89.3 FM
55,000 Watts
ALL

KTRU
Rice University
Box 1892
Houston, TX 77251
(713) 527-4098
(713) 527-4093 fax
91.7 FM
50,000 Watts
ALL

KSJL
217 Alamo Plaza, Suite 200

San Antonio, TX 78205
(210) 271-9600
(210) 271-0489 fax
96.1 FM
100,000 Watts
Urban

KTXT
Texas Tech. University
Box 4170 Tech Station
Lubbock, TX 79409
(806) 742-3916
(806) 742-3906 fax
88.1 FM 38,500 Watts
Alt.

VIRGINIA

WHRV
5200 Hampton Blvd.
Norfolk, VA 23508
(804) 489-9476
89.5 FM
50,000 Watts
Alt., Jazz

WASHINGTON

KKNW
1109 1st Ave. Suite 300
Seattle, WA 98101
106.9 FM
100,000 Watts
ALL

KNDD
100 Olive Way, Suite 1550
Seattle, WA 98101
(206) 622-3251
107.7 FM

100,000 Watts
Com. Alt

KISW
712 Aurora Ave. N
Seattle, WA 98109
(206) 285-7625
99.9 FM
100,000 Watts
Rock, Classic Rock

WISCONSIN

WWSP
University of Wisconsin/Stevens Point
101 Communications Bldg.
Stevens Point, WI 54481
(715) 346-3755
89.9 FM
11,5000 Watts
ALL, Mostly Alt.

KUWS
University of Wisconsin
1800 Grande Ave
HFAC 3160
Superior, WI 54880
(715) 394-8530
(715) 394-8404 fax
91.3 FM
84,000 Watts
Urban, Jazz, Alt.

WLFM
Lawrence University
420 W. College Ave
Appleton, WI 54912
(414) 832-6567
91.1 FM
10,500 Watts
ALL

CODES:

| T | = **This week** | **2** | = **2 weeks ago** |

4 = **4 weeks ago**

| L | = **Last week** | **3** | = **3 weeks ago** |

.... **etc.**

- = **No info on status of CD yet.**

* = We have info on the status of the CD, but there is no change this week (that we know of)   since we did not talk live to anyone.

Lm = <u>L</u>eft <u>M</u>essage, sent fax, or both

G = <u>G</u>ot CD.

A = <u>A</u>dded CD or song to playlist (commercial radio); added CD to library (non-commercial).

L = <u>L</u>ow rotation (commercial: 5-9/wk; non-comm: 4-6/wk).

M = <u>M</u>edium rotation (commercial: 10-19/wk; non-comm: 7-9/wk).

H = <u>H</u>igh rotation (commercial: 25+/wk; non-comm: 10+/wk).

S = <u>S</u>pecialty show, or te<u>s</u>ting (commercial only).

N = <u>N</u>o plays.

D = <u>D</u>iscontinue calling this station.

R = <u>R</u>esend CD.

P = Send a <u>P</u>ack for on-air giveaway: 5 CDs, 5 bio's, and 5 each of any of the other items available (posters, pictures, shirts, videos, tickets, etc.).

I = Send <u>I</u>D; You will be faxed a separate detail sheet.

V = Inter<u>V</u>iew or <u>V</u>isit. Call number provided comments column.

No Contact = The music phone, business phone, and studio phone of the station were all incapable of taking messages, and the fax did not go through. Emails, however, may have still gone through.

• Two codes in one column, for example "PL", simply means what each individual code means.

• "Station Playlist #5" means the Artist is the fifth-most-played at the station.

• "CMJ playlist #5" (non-comm only) means that the playlist information from above made it into the CMJ Magazine.

Appendix: 5

City	St	Station	T	L	2	3	4	5	6	7	8	Comments This Week

DISTRIBUTION AGREEMENT

This Distribution Agreement is made and entered into as of
_____, 2002 by and
between_____("**Firm**"),
of_____
_____ and **LABEL** of_____
_____ with reference to
the following:

WITNESSETH;

1. *(a)* **Firm** hereby engages **LABEL** as it's *(non-exclusive)* distributor in the Territory for CDs and or Cassettes presented to **LABEL** per this Agreement hereinafter called ("Records") made a part of this Agreement. *(b)* The rights herein granted to **LABEL** and the obligations of **Firm** shall be for the United States and their territories and possessions, including all U.S. Armed Forces Military Post Exchanges throughout the world ("Territory").

2. *(a)* The Term of this Agreement shall be for one (1) year of this Agreement; subject to the acceptance and approval of **LABEL** and **Firm.** *(b)* **Firm** hereby grants **LABEL** one (1) option; to renew this Agreement for a period of one (1) year. Option period shall run consecutively beginning at the expiration of the immediately preceding term of this Agreement. The renewal term option hereunder is non-automatic and mutually exercisable; in which **LABEL** or **Firm** gives written notice not to exercise such option at least ten (10) days prior to the commencement of the renewal term.

3. *(a)* For consideration and placement. **Firm** or it's Affiliates will be required to deliver a reasonable amount of promotional CD's (50-units *minimum* up to 300-units *maximum*) per title to **LABEL** of each title to be considered, for the purposes of and as a means of offsetting costs in the areas of: In-store listening CD's, retail incentives, free-goods, product placement, promotions by **LABEL**, as well as shipping and print advertising. In addition to the reasonable amount of promotional CD's, **Firm** or it's Affiliates will also be required to deliver to **LABEL** a synopsis or bio of artists(s) listing accomplishments, promotion or marketing efforts with regard to their release, radio air play, etc. in order that **LABEL** can prepare a one-sheet for retail to enter each accepted product into the system. *(b)* All projects released through **LABEL** will be distributed regionally, nationally and internationally based on promoted and targeted areas through **Firm's** and **LABEL'**

promotional efforts, which may require a **LABEL** bar code. In the event a title does have already a bar code, the **LABEL** bar code will not be necessary. Adjustments in price will be applied if CD's have no shrink wrap (*subject to reasonable manufacturing re-shrink wrap fees with approval from **LABEL** and **Firm**). Any future reorders of product to fill orders must be manufactured by **LABEL** whereby the **LABEL** bar code will be stripped in at a cost of $75.00. *(c)* **LABEL** Logo, address and web site address will be applied to **Firm's** manufactured products during subsequent product runs throughout the course of this agreement. "Shipping product to Distribution warehouse is the responsibility of **Firm**. *(d)* Any Record that shows minimal sales activity, after a period of eight (8) months may be deemed and returned to **Firm** inactive and subject to being pulled from all **LABEL** retail accounts. 'Minimal sales activity would be considered record sales of under 100 CD's and/or Cassettes in the eight (8) month period.

4. *(a)* No payment shall be made to **Firm** on the initial promotional CD's given to **LABEL** per release of each title. Payment will only begin once the first unit past 500 units is sold, verifiable through Soundscan (in conjunction to [section 4(b) see below). **LABEL** shall be entitled to (25%) of the "Net Profits" on all orders shipped for *service fee*. The service includes (Promotional services provided in this capacity)- **LABEL's** web site, internet promotions, college networks-through-out US, targeted - [posters, flyer's, record pools, reasonable radio advertising in targeted areas and music video promotion, calling buyers and sales reps on titles-promoting sales activity through-out distribution system. "Net Profits" are herein defined as gross monies received from the sale of records and received by **LABEL** from (Distributor). Monies will be held in the **LABEL** [credit] account with reference to **Firm**, bar code assigned to **Firm** per each specific title and reference accounting number. *(b)* Providing **Firm** has sold 500 units, verifiable through Soundscan, payment by **LABEL** to **Firm** shall be made on fifty percent (50%) of payments received by **LABEL**, and only on invoices paid by (Distributor), with a reserve of fifty percent (50%) to be liquidated every calendar quarter until fully liquidated in respect to (each) project-(album/single-cassette/cd) being distributed.

5. All notices hereunder shall be in writing and shall be sent by certified mail, return receipt requested to **Firm** at it's address first above written and to **LABEL** at it's address first above written.

6. LABEL and **Firm** warrants, represents and agrees that: *(a)* **LABEL** and **Firm** has the full right and power to enter into and fully perform all of its obligations under this Agreement;*(b)*

LABEL and **Firm** is not under any disability restriction or prohibition, whether contractual or otherwise, with respect to **LABEL** and **Firm's** right to execute this Agreement or **LABEL** and **Firm's** right to perform its term and conditions; *(c)* No prior obligations, contracts or agreements of any kind undertaken or entered into by **LABEL** and **Firm** will interfere in any manner with the complete performance of this Agreement by **LABEL** and **Firm**.

7. Wherever in this Agreement **Firm** 's approval or consent is required, **Firm** shall give **LABEL** written notice of approval or disapproval within ten (10) business days after such notice is received by **Firm**. In the event of disapproval or no consent, the reasons therefore shall be stated. Failure to give such notice to **LABEL** as aforesaid shall be deemed to be consent or approval.

8. Disclosure of relationship- **LABEL** and **Firm** agrees to disclose below any business or personal relationships which it may have, or any of its entities. Failure to disclose, or any fraudulent disclosure, will result in immediate cancellation of this agreement and monies due to **Firm** will be paid in full within 60 days or sooner of cancellation of agreement, along with remaining **Firm** units.

NAME   **RELATIONSHIP**
-                                   •
-                                   •
-                                   •
-                                   •

9. For the purposes of this Agreement, the following definitions shall apply: *(a)* " **LABEL** " - refers to it's principals or assigns. *(b)* " **Firm** " - refers to any promotional company, recording company, management, artist or group that is a party to this Agreement. *(c)*"Record" - The equivalent of a compact disc or cassette tape of at least 30 minutes in length intended to use in retail.

10. This Agreement sets forth the entire agreement between the parties with respect to the subject matter hereof. No modification, amendment, waiver, termination or discharge of this Agreement, shall be binding upon either party unless confirmed by a written instrument signed by an officer of the party to be charged.

11. This Agreement shall be deemed to have been made in the State of _____ and its validity, construction, performance and breach shall be governed by the laws of the State of _____ applicable to agreements made and to be wholly performed therein.

IN WITNESS WHEREOF, the parties hereto have executed this Agreement on the day and year first above written,

FIRM:

By_____
       (an authorized signatory)
Title_____
Date_____

LABEL:

By_____
       (an authorized signatory)
Title_____
Date_____

PRODUCTION, MANUFACTURE &
DISTRIBUTION AGREEMENT

This Agreement is made and entered into as of _____, 2002 by and between _____ ("**Group**"), of _____ and **LABEL** of _____ with reference to the following
WITNESSETH;

2. *(a)* **Group** hereby engages **LABEL** as its *(non-exclusive)* distributor in the Territory for the CD and or Cassette only, indicated in this Agreement hereinafter called ("Records") made a part of this Agreement *(b)* The rights herein granted to **LABEL** and the obligations of **Group** shall be for the United States and their territories and possessions, including all U.S. Armed Forces Military Post Exchanges throughout the world ("Territory"). *(c)* Further, **LABEL** will be responsible for recording/production of said album master, post-production, artwork and manufacturing.

2. *(a)* The Term of this Agreement shall be for one (2) years; subject to the acceptance and approval of **LABEL** and **Group** *(b)* **Group** hereby grants **LABEL** one (1) option; to renew this Agreement for a period of one (1) year. Option period shall run consecutively beginning at the expiration of the immediately preceding term of this Agreement. The renewal term option hereunder is non-automatic and mutually exercisable; in which **LABEL** or **Group** gives written notice not to exercise such option at least ten (10) days prior to the commencement of the renewal term.

3. *(a)* For consideration and placement. **LABEL** will be required to manufacture retail ready packaged CD's for resell as well as a reasonable amount of promotional CD's (150-units *minimum* up to 1,500-units *maximum*), for the purposes of promotion in the areas of: in-store listening CD's, retail incentives, free-goods, product placement, promotions by **LABEL**, as well as shipping and print advertising. **LABEL** is required to provide Master Recording (CDR) for this purpose as well as Master Recording including applicable artwork and graphic materials. **Group** will be required to deliver to **LABEL** a synopsis or bio of artists(s) listing accomplishments, promotion or marketing efforts with regard to their release, radio air play, etc. in order that **LABEL** can prepare a one-sheet for retail to enter the accepted product into the system.

(b) All projects released through **LABEL** will be distributed regionally and nationally based on promoted and targeted areas through **Group's** and **LABEL** promotion's efforts, which will require the **LABEL** bar code. *(c)* **LABEL** Logo, address and web site address will be applied to **Groups** manufactured products during the course of the agreement. "Shipping product to Distribution warehouse is the responsibility of **LABEL**. *(d)* Any Record that shows minimal sales activity, after a period of eight (8) months may be deemed and returned to **Group** inactive and subject to being pulled from all **LABEL** retail accounts. 'Minimal sales activity would be considered record sales of under 100 CD's and/or Cassettes in the eight (8) month period. In this instance, **Group** will have the option to buy back / purchase the existing inventory of units from **LABEL** at a rate of $1.00 each for retail ready or packaged units and .80c each for promotional units. If **Group** fails to exercise this option within 30 days, **LABEL** is granted full right to discount or dispose of inventory in any means without obligation to **Group**.

4. *(a)* No payment shall be made to **Group** on promotional use CD's manufactured by **LABEL** per release. Payment will only begin once the first retail ready unit past 500 units is sold, verifiable through Soundscan (in conjunction to [section 4(b) see below). **LABEL** shall be entitled to (35%) of the "Net Profits" on all orders shipped for *service fee*. The service fee includes (Promotional services provided in this capacity)- **LABEL's** web site, internet promotions, college networks-through-out US, targeted - [posters, flyer's, record pools, reasonable radio advertising in targeted areas and music video promotion, calling buyers and sales reps on titles- promoting sales activity through-out distribution system. This agreement is deemed to be "Production, Manufacture and Distribution" in that **LABEL** and **Group** will jointly promote, market and advertise the project for the mutual benefit of both. In this regard it is understood that **LABEL** will incur costs and expense which will be non-recoupable. **Group** agrees to aggressively maintain a performance schedule as well as incur costs related to such activity all in support of the project. **Group** further understands and agrees that it may be called upon by **LABEL** to travel to markets foreign and domestic to perform in support of the project with relative costs to be incurred by **Group**. "Net Profits" are herein defined as gross monies received from the sale of records at retail outlets and received by **LABEL** from (Distributor). Monies will be held in the **LABEL** [credit] account with reference to **Group**, bar code assigned to **Group** and reference accounting number to be accounted for and disbursed to **Group** quarterly. *(b)* Providing **Group** has sold 500 units, verifiable through Soundscan, payment by **LABEL** to **Group** shall be made at (65%) of payments received by **LABEL**, and only on invoices paid by (Distributor), to be liquidated every calendar quarter until fully liquidated in respect to (each) project-(album/single-cassette/CD) being mastered and distributed.

6.   All notices hereunder shall be in writing and shall be sent by certified mail, return receipt requested to **Group** at it's address first above written and to **LABEL** at it's address first above written.

6. **LABEL** and **Group** warrant, represent and agree that: *(a)* **LABEL** and **Group** has the full right and power to enter into and fully perform all of its obligations under this Agreement; *(b)* **LABEL** and **Group** is not under any disability restriction or prohibition, whether contractual or otherwise, with respect to **LABEL** and **Group's** right to execute this Agreement or **LABEL** and **Group's** right to perform its term and conditions; *(c)* No prior obligations, contracts or agreements of any kind undertaken or entered into by **LABEL** and **Group** will interfere in any manner with the complete performance of this Agreement by **LABEL** and **Group**.

7. Wherever in this Agreement **Group's** approval or consent is required, **Group** shall give **LABEL** written notice of approval or disapproval within ten (10) business days after such notice is received by **Group**. In the event of disapproval or no consent, the reasons therefore shall be stated. Failure to give such notice to **LABEL** as aforesaid shall be deemed to be consent or approval.

8. Disclosure of relationship- **LABEL** and **Group** agrees to disclose below any business or personal relationships which it may have, or any of its entities. Failure to disclose, or any fraudulent disclosure, will result in immediate cancellation of this agreement and monies due to **Group** will be paid in full within 60 days or sooner of cancellation of agreement, along with remaining **Group** units.

NAME	RELATIONSHIP
•	•
•	•

9. For the purposes of this Agreement, the following definitions shall apply: *(a)* " LABEL " - refers to it's principals or assigns. *(b)* "Group" - refers to any recording company, management, artist or group that is a party to this Agreement. *(c)*"Record" - The equivalent of a compact disc or cassette tape of at least 30 minutes in length intended to use in retail.

10. This Agreement sets forth the entire agreement between the parties with respect to the subject matter hereof. No modification, amendment, waiver, termination or discharge of this Agreement, shall be binding upon either party unless confirmed by a written instrument signed by an officer of the party to be charged.

11. This Agreement shall be deemed to have been made in the State of _____ and its validity, construction, performance and breach shall be governed by the laws of the State of _____ applicable to agreements made and to be wholly performed therein.

IN WITNESS WHEREOF, the parties hereto have executed this Agreement on the day and year first above written,

LABEL:
By_____
　　　　　(an authorized signatory)
Title_____
Date_____

GROUP:
By_____
　　　　　(an authorized signatory)
Title_____
Date_____

Appendix: 8

ARTIST MANAGEMENT AGREEMENT

This Agreement is made and entered into as of
_____, 2002 by and between
_____
("Artist/Musician")_____
_____ _____ and _____ of
_____ with reference to the following:

WITNESSETH;
1. Scope of Agreement- *_Artist_ will be referred to as _Musician_ in this letter of Agreement._ Musician hereby employs Agent and Agent hereby accepts employment as Musician _exclusive booking agent_, manager and representative throughout the world with respect to musician's services, appearances and endeavors as an artist. As used in this agreement "Musician" refers to the undersigned musician and to musicians performing with any orchestra or group which Musician leads or conducts and whom Musician shall make subject to the terms of this agreement; "A.F.M." refers to the American Federation of Musicians of the United States and Canada.

2. Duties of Agent
(a) Agent agrees to use reasonable efforts in the performance of the following duties: assist Musician in obtaining, obtain offers of, and negotiate, engagements for Musician', advise, aid. counsel and guide Musician with respect to Musician's professional career; promote and publicize Musician's name and tatenis; carry on business correspondence in Musician's behalf relating to Musician's professional career, cooperate with duly constituted and authorized representatives of Musician in the performance of such duties.
(b) Agent will maintain office, staff and facilities reasonably adequate for the rendition of such services.
(c) Agent will not accept any engagements for Musician without Musician's prior approval which shall not be unreasonably withheld.
(d) Agent shall fully comply with all applicable laws, rules and regulations of governmental authorities and secure such licenses as may be required for the rendition of services hereunder.

3. Rights of Agent
(a) Agent may render similar services to others and may engage in other businesses and ventures, subject, however, to the limitations imposed by below.

131

(b) Musician will promptly refer to Agent all communications, written or oral received by or on behalf of Musician relating to the services and appearances fav Musician.

(c) Without Agent's written consent. Musician will not engage *any* other person, firm or corporation to perform the services to be performed by Agent hereunder (except that Musician may employ a personal manager) nor will Musician perform or appear professionally or offer so to do except through Agent.

(d) Agent may publicize the fact that Agent is the exclusive booking agent and representative for Musician.

(c) Agent shall have the right to use or to permit others to use Musician's name and likeness in advertising or publicity relating to Musician's services and appearances bill without cost or expense to Musician unless Musician shall otherwise specifically agree in writing.

(f) In the event of Musician's breach of this agreement. Agent's sole right and remedy for such breach shall be the receipt from Musician of the commissions specified in this agreement, but only if, as. and when. Musician receives moneys or other consideration on which such commissions are payable hereunder.

4. Compensation of Agent

(a) In consideration of the services to be rendered by Agent hereunder. Musician agrees to pay to Agent commissions equal lo the percentages, set forth below, of the gross moneys received by Musician, directly or indirectly, for each engagement on which commissions are payable hereunder:

(1) *Fifteen percent (15%)* if the duration of the engagement is *two(2)* or more consecutive days per week.

(2) *Twenty percent (20%)* for Single Miscellaneous Engagements of *one (1) day* duration—each for a different employer in a different location.

(3) In no event, however, shall the payment of any such commissions result in the retention by Musician for any engagement of net moneys or other consideration in an amount less than the applicable minimum scale of the A.F.M. or of any local thereof having jurisdiction over such engagement.

(4) In no event shall the payment of any such commissions result in the receipt by Agent for any engagement of commissions, fees or other consideration, directly, or indirectly. from any person or persons, including the Musician, which in aggregate exceed the commissions provided for in this agreement. Any commission, fee. or other consideration received by

Agent from any source other than Musician, directly or indirectly, on account of. as a result of. or in connection with supplying the services of Musician shall be reported to Musician and the amount thereof shall be deducted from the commissions payable by the Musician hereunder.

(b) Commissions shall become due and payable to Agent immediately following the receipt thereof by Musician or by anyone else in Musician's behalf.

(c) No commissions shall be payable on any engagement if Musician is not paid for such engagement irrespective of the reasons for such non-payment of Musician, including but not limited to non-payment by reason of the fault of Musician. This shall not preclude the awarding of damages by the International Executive Board to a booking agent lo compensate him for actual expenses incurred as the direct result of the cancellation of an engagement when such cancellation was the fault of the member.

(d) Agent's commissions shall be payable on all moneys or other considerations received by Musician pursuant io contracts for engagements negotiated or entered into during the term of this agreement: *if specifically agreed by Musician by initiating the margin hereof,* to contracts for engagements in existence at the commencement of the term hereof (excluding, however, any engagements a» to which Musician is under prior obligation to pay commissions to:

(1)   If Artist shall so request and shall simultaneously furnish Agent with the data relating to deductions, the Agent within 45 days following the end of each 12 months period during the term of this agreement and within 45 days following the termination of this Agreement, shall account to and furnish Musician with a detailed statement Itemizing the gross amounts received for all engagements during the period to which such liccounting relates, the moneys or other considerations upon which Agent's commissions are based, and the amount of rents commissions resulting from such computations. Upon request, a copy of such statement shall be furnished promptly to the Office of the President of the A.F.M.

(2)   Any balances owed by or to the parties shall be paid as follows: by the Agent at the time of rendering such statement; by the Musician within 30 days after receipt of such statement.

5. Duration and termination of Agreement

(a) The term of this agreement shall be as stated in the opening heading hereof, subject to termination as provided in Section(b), 6 and 10 below.

(b) In addition to termination pursuant to other provisions of this agreement, this agreement may be terminated by either partly, by notice as provided below, if Musician:

(1) is unemployed for four *(4) consecutive weeks* at any time during the term hereof; or

(2) does not obtain employment for at least *twenty (20) cumulative weeks* of engagements to be performed during each of the first and second *six (6) months* periods during the term hereof; or

(3) does not obtain employment for at least forty (40) cumulative weeks of engagements to be performed during each subsequent year of the term hereof.

(c) Notice of such termination shall be given by certified mail addressed to the addressee at his last known address and a copy thereof shall be sent to the A.F.M. Such termination shall be effective as of the dale of mailing of such notice if and when approved by the A.F.M. Such notice shall be mailed no later than *two (2) weeks* following the occurrence of any event described in:

(1) above: *two (2) weeks* following a period in excess of *thirteen (13)* of the cumulative weeks of unemployment specified in (2) above; and two (2) weeks following a period in excess of twenty-six (26) of the cumulative weeks of unemployment specified in (3) above. Failure to give notice as aforesaid shall constitute a waiver *of* the right to terminate based upon the happening of such prior events,

(d) Musician's disability resulting in failure to perform engagements and Musician's unreasonable refusal to accept and perform engagements shall not by themselves either deprive Agent of it's right to or give Musician the right to terminate (as provided in (b) above).

(e) As used in this agreement, a "week" shall commence on Sunday and terminate on Saturday. A "week of engagements" shall mean any one of the following:

(1) a week during which Musician is to perform on at least *four (4) days*; or

(2) a week during which Musician's gross earnings equals or exceeds the lowest such gross earnings obtained by Musician for performances rendered during any one of the immediately preceding *six (6) weeks*; or

(3) a week during which Musician)s to perform engagements on commercial television or radio or in concert for compensation equal at least to *three (3)*

134

times the minimum scales of the A.F.M. or of any local thereof having jurisdiction applicable to such engagements.

6. Agent's maintenance of A.F.M. booking agent Agreement

Agent represents that Agent is presently a party to an A.F.M. Booking Agent Agreement which is in full force and effect. If such A.F.M. Booking Agent Agreement shall terminate, the rights of the parties hereunder shall be governed by the terms and conditions of said Booking Agent Agreement relating to the effect of termination of such agreements which are incorporated herein by reference.

7. No other Agreements

This is the only and the complete agreement between the parties relating to all or any part of the subject matter covered by this Agreement. There is no other agreement, arrangement or participation between the parties, nor do the parties stand in any relationship to each other which is not created by this agreement, whereby the terms and conditions of this agreement are avoided or evaded, directly or indirectly or such as, by way of example but not limitation, contracts, arrangements. relationships or participation's relating to publicity services, business management, personal management of music publishing, or instruction.

8. Incorporation of A.F.M. by-laws, etc.

There are incorporated into and made part of this agreement, as though fully set forth herein, the present and future provisions of the By-laws, Rules, Regulations and Resolutions of the A.F.M. and those of its locals which do not conflict therewith. The parties acknowledge their responsibility to be fully acquainted, now and for the duration of this agreement, with the contents thereof.

9. Submission and determination of disputes

Every claim, dispute, controversy or difference arising out of, dealing with, relating to, or affecting the interpretation or application of this agreement, or the violation or breach, or the threatened violation or breach thereof shall be submitted, heard and determined by the International Executive Board of the A.F.M., in accordance with the rules of such Board (regardless of the termination or purported termination of this agreement or of the Agent's A.F.M. Booking Agent Agreement), and such determination shall be conclusive, final and binding on the parties.

10. No assignment of this agreement

This agreement shall be personal to the parties and shall not be transferable or assignable by operation of law or otherwise without the prior consent of the Musician and of the A.F.M. The obligations imposed by this agreement shall be binding upon the parties. The Musician may terminate this agreement at any lime within _ninety (90) days_ after the transfer of a controlling interest in the Agent.

11. Negotiation for renewal

Neither party shall enter into negotiations for or agree to the renewal or extension of this agreement prior to the beginning of the final year of the term hereof.

12. Approval by A.F.M.

This agreement shall not become effective unless, within _thirty (30) days_ following its execution, an executed copy thereof is filed with and is thereafter approved in writing by the A.F.M.

IN WITNESS WHEREOF,
The parties hereto have executed this agreement the _____day of _____, 2002

Agent

Artist "Group"

Appendix: 9

Rank #	Market	Population	% Black	% Latin	% Asian
1	New York	15.3 Million	16.6	18.2	7.2
2	Los Angeles	10.3 Million	7.7	38.1	13.3
3	Chicago, IL	7.2 Million	18.3	12.9	4.2
4	San Francisco	5.8 Million	7.9	17.9	19.4
5	Dallas - Ft. Worth	4.3 Million	13.3	14.5	3.7
6	Philadelphia, PA	4.2 Million	18.9	4.1	3.1
7	Detroit, MI	3.9 Million	21.4	2.2	1.9
8	Boston, MA	3.8 Million	5.6	5.2	4.2
9	Washington, DC	3.8 Million	25.2	7.5	6.9
10	Houston - Galveston, TX	3.7 Million	17.3	22.7	5.1
11	Atlanta, GA	3.5 Million	24.8	3.4	2.8
12	Miami - Ft. Lauderdale, FL	3.4 Million	16.3	38.4	1.9
13	Puerto Rico	3.2 Million	no data	no data	no data
14	Seattle - Tacoma, WA	2.9 Million	4.6	4	4
15	Phoenix, AZ	2.65 Million	3.6	17.2	2.4
16	Minneapolis - St. Paul, MN	2.45 Million	4.2	1.9	3.6
17	San Diego, Ca	2.4 Million	5.1	24.3	10.7
18	Nassau - Suffolk	2.36 Million	7.4	7.7	3.5
19	St. Louis, MO	2.12 Million	17	1.3	1.3
20	Baltimore, MD	2.1 Million	26.9	1.7	2.5
21	Tampa - St. Petersburg, FL	2.1 Million	9.2	9	1.7
22	Denver - Boulder, CO	2.03 Million	5.1	12.6	3
23	Pittsburgh, PA	2 Million	8	0.7	1
24	Portland, OR	1.84 Million	2.6	5.4	4.3
25	Cleveland, OH	1.76 Million	18.3	2.6	1.4
26	Cincinnati, OH	1.63 Million	11	0.6	1
27	Sacramento, CA	1.54 Million	7.3	31	5
28	Riverside - San Bernardino, CA	1.5 Million	7.3	31	5
29	Kansas City	1.47 Million	12.7	3.5	1.5
30	San Jose, CA	1.43 Million	3.2	24	21.9
31	San Antonio, TX	1.42 Million	5.7	50.6	1.7
32	Milwaukee - Racine, WI	1.39 Million	13.7	4.3	1.7
33	Middlesex - Somerset, NJ	1.36 Million	no data	no data	no data
34	Salt Lake City, UT	1.35 Million	1	6.9	2.8
35	Providence, RI	1.34 Million	2.9	4.9	2.2
36	Columbus, OH	1.33 Million	12.5	1	2
37	Charlotte - Gastonia, NC	1.3 Million	19.4	1.7	1.6
38	Norfolk, VA	1.24 Million	29	2.9	3.5
39	Orlando, FL	1.23 Million	13.1	12.1	3
40	Indianapolis, IN	1.2 Million	13.5	1.2	1.1

41	Las Vegas, NV	1.2 Million	9.1	15.7	4.9
42	Greensboro - Winston Salem, NC	1.09 Million	18.8	1.3	1
43	Austin, TX	1.07 Million	9.2	23.5	3.1
44	Nashville, TN	1.05 Million	15.2	1.3	1.5
45	New Orleans, LA	1.05 Million	32.8	5.2	2.3
46	Raleigh - Durham, NC	1.04 Million	23.2	2.3	2.6
47	West Palm Beach, FL	1.01 Million	12.4	9.9	1.6
48	Memphis, TN	1 Million	39.9	1.3	1.1
49	Hartford - New Britain, CT	1 Million	8.1	7.8	7.8
50	Buffalo - Niagara Falls, NY	976,500	10.8	2.3	1.3
51	Monmouth - Ocean, NJ	973,200	6.2	4.7	3
52	Jacksonville, FL	948,400	21.4	3.4	2.6
53	Rochester, NY	911,700	8.8	3.4	1.9
54	Oaklahoma City, OK	904,000	9.9	4.3	2.2
55	Louisville, KY	895,500	12.2	0.8	0.8
56	Richmond, VA	847,800	29.1	1.5	1.9
57	Birmingham, AL	836,500	26.3	0.7	0.5
58	Dayton, OH	825,400	13.4	0.8	1.3
59	Westchester, NY	797,800	no data	no data	no data
60	Greenville - Spartanburg, SC	783,200	16.9	1	0.9
61	Albany - Schenectady - Troy, NY	738,000	4.6	2	1.8
62	Honolulu	730,400	3.3	6.5	64.6
63	McAllen - Brownsville, TX	727,600	0.2	85.1	0.4
64	Tucson, AZ	722,600	3.3	26.2	2.4
65	Tulsa, OK	704,700	7.5	2.5	1.1
66	Grand Rapids, MI	666,000	6	3.6	1.6
67	Wilkes Barre - Scranton, PA	652,100	1.1	1.1	0.8
68	Fresno, CA	636,600	4.3	40.3	10.7
69	Allentown - Bethlehem, PA	631,700	1.9	4.9	1.6
70	Ft. Meyers - Naples, FL	624,200	5.8	9.4	0.8
71	Knoxville, TN	598,000	6.1	0.8	1.1
72	Albuquerque, NM	590,700	3	36.8	2
73	Akron, OH	586,200	10.4	0.7	1.2
74	Wilmington, DE	551,400	16.1	3.2	1.9
75	Monterey - Salinas, CA	546,800	3.4	32.3	8.3
76	El Paso, TX	545,200	3.1	73	1.5
77	Harrisburg - Lebanon, PA	537,200	7	2.1	1.6
78	Sarasota - Bradenton, FL	534,800	6	3.9	0.9
79	Syracuse, NY	534,800	5.8	1.6	1.7
80	Omaha - Council Bluffs, NE	521,200	8.2	4.6	1.7
81	Toledo, OH	509,900	11.4	3.6	1.3
82	Springfield, MA	509,600	6.3	8.4	2.1
83	Baton Rouge, LA	493,200	30.1	1.7	1.4

84	Greenville - New Bern, NC	490,300	25.5	3.6	1.5
85	Little Rock, AR	490,300	19.8	1.8	0.8
86	Gainsville - Ocala, FL	459,700	16.4	4.5	2.2
87	Stockton, CA	459,000	4.8	27.4	15.8
88	Columbia, SC	459,700	28.5	1.7	1.4
89	Des Moines, IA	453,800	3.6	2.4	2.7
90	Bakersfield, CA	453,100	5.5	35.4	4.6
91	Mobile, AL	450,500	26.5	1.3	0.9
92	Witchita, KS	450,000	7.4	5	2.4
93	Charleston, SC	446,500	29.7	1.9	1.7
94	Spokane, WA	444,900	1.2	2.5	2.1
95	Daytona Beach, FL	441,000	10	5	1.2
96	Colorado Springs, CO	434,800	6.7	9.8	3.4
97	Madison, WI	429,300	3.2	2	3.2
98	Johnson City - Kingsport, TN	419,200	2.2	0.6	0.4
99	Lakeland - Winter Haven, FL	416,000	14.2	5.1	1
100	Melbourne - Titusville, FL	414,900	8.7	4.3	2.2
101	Ft. Wayne, IN	396,800	6.8	2.1	0.9
102	Lexington - Fayette, KY	412,600	9.7	1	1.5
103	Lafayette, LA	411,300	27.2	1.7	1.1
104	New Haven, CT	410,600	12.6	6	2
105	Morristown, NJ	409,000	3.3	6.1	6.2
106	Chattanooga, TN	406,900	13.5	1	1
107	York, PA	404,300	3	1.8	0.9
108	Youngstown - Warren, OH	403,000	11.5	1.7	0.6
109	Roanoke - Lynchburg, VA	389,500	15.9	0.9	0.8
110	Bridgeport, CT	398,200	9.7	11.4	2.9
111	Visalia - Tulare - Hanford, CA	394,700	3.1	42	5.6
112	Augusta, GA	376,300	31.8	2.2	2.2
113	Lancaster, PA	392,100	2.2	4.4	1.6
114	Santa Rosa, CA	390,200	1.3	12.9	3.8
115	Oxnard - Ventura, CA	386,900	2.6	40.3	6.8
116	Huntsville, AL	385,400	17	1.5	1.6
117	Ft. Pierce - Stuart, FL	382,800	12.1	5.1	1
118	Worcester, MA	381,500	2.3	5	2.4
119	Portsmouth - Dover, NH	372,300	0.7	1.1	1.3
120	Lansing - East Lansing, MI	372,500	7.2	4.3	2.7
121	Boise, ID	366,600	0.5	7.2	1.5
122	Jackson, MS	365,200	41.1	0.6	0.6
123	Modesto, CA	360,800	1.6	25.6	6.8
124	Flint, MI	357,600	20.1	2.2	0.9
125	Pensacola, FL	350,600	16.9	2.5	2.7
126	Fayetteville, NC	345,900	27.3	6	2.5
127	Reno, NV	342,500	2.3	12	5

128	Canton, OH	341,200	6.8	0.9	0.5
129	Saginaw - Bay City, MI	331,700	9.5	4.8	0.9
130	Ft. Collins, CO	331,700	3.7	2.3	2.3
131	Reading, PA	319,800	3	5.7	1.4
132	Shreveport, LA	319,000	34.6	1.4	0.8
133	Beaumont - Port Arthur, TX	317,400	23.8	5.1	2.2
134	Corpus Christi, TX	306,800	3.8	56.1	1.2
135	Atlantic City, NJ	303,900	14.6	6.9	2.6
136	Biloxi - Gulfport, MS	302,000	18.8	2	2.4
137	Trenton, NJ	300,700	19.1	7.4	4.6
138	Stamford - Norwalk, CT	300,000	10.3	8.3	3.2
139	Appleton, WI	298,600	0.6	0.9	1.7
140	Quad Cities, IA - IL	296,600	5.4	4.9	1
141	Burlington, VT	127,400	1.1	1.4	1.8
142	Peoria, IL	286,700	7	1.3	1.1
143	Newburgh - Middletown, NY	281,300	6.9	8.4	1.7
144	Springfield, MO	280,300	1.6	0.9	0.8
145	Ann Arbor, MI	279,300	11.7	2.4	5.8
146	Tyler - Longview, TX	278,800	20.4	5.7	0.7
147	Montgomery, AL	265,600	35.2	1	0.7
148	Eugene - Springfield, OR	275,600	0.7	3.4	2.4
149	Fayetteville, AR	272,300	1	3.1	0.9
150	Salisbury - Ocean City, MD	271,600	24.1	1.4	0.9
151	Huntington - Ashland, WV - KY	267,800	2.2	0.4	0.4
152	Rockford, IL	267,700	8.2	4.2	1.5
153	Macon, GA	260,000	37.2	1.8	1.2
154	Killeen - Temple, TX	253,100	18	14.5	4.4
155	Evansville, IN	248,100	6	0.7	0.6
156	Utica - Rome, NY	247,700	4.4	2.6	1.1
157	Flagstaff - Prescott, AZ	237,000	no data	no data	no data
158	Palm Springs, CA	244,100	2.3	39.3	4.7
159	Savannah, GA	242,600	35.8	1.9	1.5
160	Poughkeepsie, NY	238,100	8.3	4.7	3.3
161	Erie, PA	232,800	5.6	1.4	0.7
162	Portland, ME	226,600	0.7	0.8	1.1
163	Fredericksburg, VA	226,000	no data	no data	no data
164	Tallahassee, FL	226,000	26	3.3	2
165	New Bedford, MA	223,600	2.4	3.9	1.4
166	Hagerstown - Chambersburg, MD	222,800	5.1	1	0.8
167	South Bend, IN	222,200	9.9	2.6	1.4
168	Wausau - Stevens Point, WI	221,500	0.2	0.6	2.2
169	Myrtle Beach, SC	219,900	21.8	1	0.9
170	New London, CT	205,400	4.8	3.9	2.2
171	Ft. Smith, AR	213,500	3.7	2.3	2.3
172	Charleston, WV	213,500	5.3	0.5	0.6

173	San Luis Obispo, CA	213,000	1.9	16.3	3.8
174	Lincoln, NE	212,700	2.3	3	2.5
175	Binghamton, NY	209,300	1.7	1.4	2.2
176	Anchorage, AK	207,900	5.1	4.6	6.2
177	Wilmington, NC	207,600	18.8	1.4	0.7
178	Columbus, GA	204,000	39.5	4.4	2
179	Kalamazoo, MI	199,700	8.9	1.9	2
180	Lubbock, TX	199,400	7.7	25.4	1.8
181	Asheville, NC	198,100	7.4	1.2	0.7
182	Johnstown, PA	197,000	1.9	0.7	0.3
183	Tupelo, MS	195,600	20.6	0.6	0.2
184	Cape Cod, MA	195,600	1.7	1.3	0.8
185	Green Bay, WI	188,900	0.6	0.9	1.8
186	Topeka, KS	187,000	6.3	5.3	0.9
187	Odessa - Midland, TX	186,700	6.3	28.5	1.1
188	Dothan, AL	180,400	20.2	1.5	1
189	Manchester, NH	185,300	0.6	2	1.4
190	Yakima, WA	181,200	1.2	27.6	1.8
191	Amarillo, TX	180,500	5.6	14.7	2.6
192	Traverse City, MI	169,700	0.2	0.9	0.5
193	Waco, TX	178,700	15.4	13.9	1
194	Danbury, CT	178,400	2.3	4.1	2.9
195	Morgantown, WV	177,600	2.2	0.9	1.1
196	Merced, CA	177,000	4	34.9	9.9
197	Terre Haute, IN	172,600	3.1	0.7	0.8
198	Clarksville, TN	172,300	no data	no data	no data
199	Chico, CA	171,700	1.2	9.1	3.9
200	Santa Barbara, CA	168,800	2.2	27.1	5.9
201	Santa Maria - Lompoc, CA	168,500	2.5	34.7	5.9
202	Springfield, IL	168,800	7.7	1	1
203	Frederick, MD	165,700	7	1.6	1.4
204	Cedar Rapids, IA	162,400	1.9	1.4	1.1
205	Bowling Green, KY	161,400	2.4	0.7	0.6
206	Florence, SC	160,900	38.1	0.6	0.3
207	Medford - Ashland, OR	156,400	0.2	5.2	1.3
208	Elmira, NY	156,000	3.5	1.3	1
209	Tri-Cities, WA	155,700	1.7	15.6	2.8
210	Laredo, TX	154,500	0.2	94.8	0.5
211	Sioux Falls, SD	146,900	0.6	0.6	0.8
212	Champaign, IL	143,300	9.9	2.4	6
213	Bangor, ME	151,700	0.8	1.1	0.8
214	Alexandria, LA	152,500	27.5	1.6	0.7
215	Lake Charles, LA	149,800	24.3	1.4	0.5
216	Laurel - Hattiesburg, MS	147,400	24.5	0.8	0.6
217	Fargo - Moorhead, ND - MN	146,700	0.4	1.4	1.4
218	Blacksburg, VA	146,000	4.9	1.3	2.9
219	Ft. Walton Beach, FL	143,600	9.8	4.3	4.1
220	St. Cloud, MN	141,700	0.7	0.6	0.9
221	Tuscaloosa, AL	138,400	26.3	0.8	1

222	Muskegon, MI	137,900	no data	no data	no data
223	Duluth, MN	135,700	0.9	0.8	0.8
224	Winchester, VA	138,900	4.8	1.1	0.7
225	Charlottesville, VA	138,500	15.8	1.4	2.7
226	Marion - Carbondale, IL	138,000	5	1.4	2.1
227	Redding, CA	135,200	0.7	4.8	2.5
228	Rochester, MN	129,000	no data	no data	no data
229	Joplin, MO	133,700	1.1	1	0.7
230	Dubuque, IA	133,000	0.3	0.6	0.6
231	Abilene, TX	131,600	5.8	15.5	1.6
232	Bryan-College Station, TX	130,700	10.9	15.6	4.8
233	Wheeling, WV	130,500	1.9	0.5	0.4
234	Lafayette, IN	129,200	2.3	2.1	4.8
235	Bloomington, IL	129,000	4.3	1.6	1.7
236	Parkersburg - Marietta, WV - OH	127,100	1	0.4	0.4
237	Lima, OH	126,600	8.5	1.1	0.7
238	Santa Fe, NM	126,200	0.8	43.9	1.1
239	Waterloo, IA	126,100	5.7	0.9	1
240	Panama City, FL	125,800	12	2.4	2.8
241	Meadville - Franklin, PA	123,700	no data	no data	no data
242	Eau Claire, WI	123,400	0.3	0.4	2.4
243	St. George, UT	122,900	no data	no data	no data
244	Florence - Muscle Shoals, AL	121,900	no data	no data	no data
245	State College, PA	120,100	2.6	1.5	4.5
246	Pueblo, CO	120,000	2	37.7	0.8
247	Monroe, LA	119,300	31.1	0.9	0.7
248	Sussex, NJ	119,100	1.3	3.1	1.5
249	Elizabeth City, NC	116,100	2.4	0.7	0.6
250	Wichita Falls, TX	116,900	9.3	9.4	2.2
251	Columbia, MO	116,200	8.2	1.4	3.8
252	Battle Creek, MI	114,400	11.1	2.1	1.1
253	Altoona, PA	108,500	1	0.4	0.4
254	Billings, MT	107,800	0.6	2.6	0.6
255	Texarkana, TX - AR	107,800	22.4	2	0.5
256	Columbus - Starkville, MS	103,800	no data	no data	no data
257	Sioux City, IA	101,300	1.4	4.6	2
258	Williamsport, PA	99,900	2.4	0.7	0.6
259	Grand Junction, CO	98,900	0.3	8.7	0.9
260	Augusta - Waterville, ME	97,700	0.3	0.6	0.6
261	Albany, GA	95,200	46.8	1.4	0.7
262	Decatur, IL	95,100	12	no data	no data
263	Harrisonburg, VA	94,700	3.7	1.6	1
264	Mankato - New Ulm, MN	93,600	no data	no data	no data
265	Bluefield, WV	93,200	4.8	0.4	0.6
266	Lawton, OK	91,500	16.2	7.9	3.6
267	Watertown, NY	90,000	6.7	4	1.3
268	Rapid City, SD	87,200	1.9	2.5	1.5

269	Lewiston - Auburn, ME	85,500	0.5	1.1	0.7
270	San Angelo, TX	85,200	4	28.5	1.5
271	Ithaca, NY	83,500	3.6	2.6	7.2
272	Cookeville, TN	81,900	1.3	0.8	0.9
273	Bismarck, ND	78,300	0.1	0.5	0.6
274	Sebring, FL	78,100	2.4	0.7	0.6
275	Grand Forks, ND - MN	77,700	1.4	2.8	1.4
276	Jackson, TN	77,700	31.3	0.6	0.5
277	Owensboro, KY	75,800	4.1	0.3	0.4
278	Jonesboro, AR	70,400	no data	no data	no data
279	Mason City, IA	93,200	no data	no data	no data
280	Beckley, WV	67,800	7.4	0.6	0.6
281	Cheyenne, WY	66,900	2.7	9.4	1.5
282	Great Falls, MT	64,800	1.4	1.7	1.1
283	Meridian, MS	63,800	34.5	0.7	0.7
284	Brunswick, GA	56,900	27.6	1.6	0.8
285	Casper, WY	53,700	0.8	3.2	0.6

Glossary of Music and Industry Related Terms

Ad schedule – Schedule of advertising spots, usually referring to radio. Ex. 60, 30 second spots to run 15 per day from Friday through Monday.

Add – Radio play term refers to when a station officially adds a track to the playlist.

AFIM – American Federation of Independent Musicians

BDS – Broadcast Data Systems, BDS monitors radio and television broadcasts, identifying songs and commercials as they are being aired.

Broadcast corporations – Large corporations owning sometimes hundreds of radio stations of multiple formats.

Buy-in – Sales terminology meaning essentially to submit a purchase order from retail to wholesale with terms not cash.

Buzz – "Creating a buzz", generating a level of consumer awareness and interest in a release.

Call letters – Radio term for identifying insignia of a station; i.e., KMEL or WNUR.

Commercial radio – For profit radio stations. These are generally the largest and most popular stations in a market, but not always.

Co-op – Typically referring to structured arrangements with retail to prominently place, promote and push a particular title inside the store throughout a region.

Cutouts – Previously released, dated and deeply discounted music product re-packaged and re-released.

DAT – Digital Audio Tape, the preferred media for storing and manipulating audio during the recording and production process.

Disbursement schedule – Stated in the Distribution Agreement, it is the timeline and terms of which payment will be remitted.

EP – Extended play retail music single.

Fulfillment – The act of responding to purchase orders submitted by retail.

Genre – Meaning category (of music), i.e. Pop, R&B, Rap, Country, Ska, etc.

Indie – Short for independent, generally referring to independent record labels or artists.
In-store – Promotional term referring to promotional appearance inside a retail music store location.

Listening post – A listening station or device inside retail outlets facilitating the review of selected music titles for sale.

Market – Terminology defining a particular city or cluster of closely neighboring cities.

MD – Music Director (radio)

Media – Platforms for storing or conveying recorded music to listeners and consumers; i.e. compact disc, vinyl, cassette, etc.

Mix-show – Radio segments or time slots generally programmed by individual DJs incorporating mixes of many tracks.

Mom & pops – Reference to independently owned and operated music retail outlets.

MRI – Music and Recording Industry

Muze, Inc. -

NAIRD - National Association of Independent Record Distributors.

NARM – National Association of Recording Merchandisers.

Non-comm radio – Non-commercial radio, college, NPR (non-profit radio), community radio.

One sheet – Reference sheet used to detail one title containing all the pertinent data for that title; i.e. artist name, title, production credits, marketing plans, UPC number, wholesale info., artist bio, etc. Commonly used industry wide by retail buyers and distributor sales staffs.

One stop – Regional distributor or fulfillment house typically servicing smaller independent retail establishments within a region.

Pass through dollars

PD – Program Director, radio personnel.

Phonolog - Published by Muze, Inc. it is a comprehensive loose-leaf catalog that lists currently available recordings cross-referenced by label, title, artist, and category.

Playlist – Radio term, it is the track list representing a stations core music titles played; generally 20 to 30 track total.

POP – Promotional items; i.e. posters, flyers, decals, postcards, etc.

POS – Acronym for point-of-sale. The point at which product is sold to its end user. (retail stores)

Print media – Meaning magazines, newspapers, hard-copy trade publications.

Product placement – Term used to describe placement of music product at retail.

145

Product platform - Term used for any medium or format used to host music for the purpose of selling at retail; i.e. CDs, cassette, vinyl, etc.

Purchase order – Document showing order or request for product by retail.

Rack jobber - The jobber rents space for racks and bins from the retailer for a flat monthly fee. The jobber offers complete servicing of the area and retains all the money collected from sales. The jobber pays the host store a percentage of sales. Ex. Handleman Co. (K-Mart), Anderson Merchandisers (Wal-Mart).

Radio clean – Indicates that a track is edited of explicit content and ready for radio.

Radio friendly – Indicates that a track is well suited musically for radio play just as "club friendly" indicates a track is suited for dancing and club enjoyment.

Region – Cluster of markets, states; i.e. southeastern US, or the mid-west.

Regular rotation – Having made the playlist at a radio station, defined as 9 to 25 spins per week at a given station.

Retail promotion - Pushing product titles to retail Buyers and Account Reps in order to get them to "buy-in" or place your product on the shelves of their P.O.S. (point of sale) outlets.

Retail systems – Internal inventory management and tracking systems used by retail companies.

Returns – Product placed at retail that has failed to sell through and is returned to the distributor by retail companies.

RIAA – Recording Industry Association of America.

ROI – Return on investment.

Royalty – Payment made to an artist, writer or composer for each copy of a work sold at retail.

Sell through – What occurs when product placed at retail is purchased by the end user, customer.

Shrinkage – Term used by retail referring to product lost or unaccounted for after inventory count as a result of theft primarily.

Snippets – Promotional tool used for giveaways to potential consumers consisting of all the tracks of an album reduced to short samples. (60 to 90 seconds)

Soundscan - Online information system that tracks actual music product sales throughout the Unites States.

Spin rate – The per day or per week spin count on radio for a particular track. How many times the track is played on the air.

146

SRP – Suggested retail price.

Street team – Independent promotions firm. Street teams spread POP at the street level to generate consumer demand and awareness for music product releases.

Trades – Refers to music industry publications; i.e. Billboard, Radio & Records (R&R), CMJ, etc.

Units – Term used to refer to individual product item. Ex., 1,000 CDs, referred to as 1,000 units.

UPC – Universal product code; bar code.

Volume economics - Acceptance or realization of a lessor margin with the expectation of profiting more substantially overall by moving greater volume.